Ninja Foodi Ultimate Cookbook 2021

1000-Days Easy & Delicious Air Fry, Broil, Pressure Cook, Slow Cook, Dehydrate, and More Recipes for Beginners and Advanced Users

Kathleen Butts

TABLE OF CONTENTS

Chapter 5-Fish and Seafood Recipes 72

Chapter 6-Vegan and Vegetarian Recipes 85

Chapter 7-Desserts Recipes 100

Ninja Foodi Pressure Cooker and Air Fryer

The Ninja Foodi Deluxe—the deluxe pressure cooker that crisps. 9 functions: Pressure Cook, Air Fry/Air Crisp, Steam, Slow Cook, Yogurt, Sear/Saute, Bake/Roast, Broil, Dehydrate. Deluxe cooking capacity - XL 8-quart pot, XL 5-quart Cook & Crisp Basket and Deluxe Reversible Rack let you cook for a small group. TenderCrisp Technology lets you quickly pressure cook ingredients to lock in juices, then give them a crispy, golden air-fryer finish. Deluxe Reversible Rack lets you steam and broil, as well as TenderCrisp up to 8 chicken breasts at once or add servings to layered 360 meals. XL 8-quart ceramic-coated pot: Nonstick, PTFE/PFOA free, and easy to hand-wash. XL 5-quart Cook & Crisp Basket: Large-capacity, ceramic-coated, PTFE/PFOA-free nonstick basket is dishwasher safe and holds up to a 7-lb. chicken to feed your whole family.

You will change your whole life by using a Ninja Foodi, which is really the most multi-functional kitchen appliance in this world now! Everyone should have one!

Ninja Foodi Ultimate Cookbook 2021 will help you save your precious time and money regarding cooking your favorite dishes! You are going to have your nutritional and delicious recipes in a short time! This book is the perfect companion of your Ninja Foodi cooking!

This Ninja Foodi can accomplish this feat, thanks to the crisping lid that comes attached with the Foodi itself. When needed, this particular lid alongside the Air Crisp Function and Crisping Basket allows the users to seamless Air Fry their dishes and give them a satisfying crispy finish!

Welcome, to the world of amazing Ninja Foodi cooking!

The Functions of Ninja Foodi

With the TenderCrisp tech out of the way, let me talk a little bit about the different buttons and features found in the Foodi. The following guide should help you understand what each of the buttons does and how you can use them to their fullest extent.

Pressure

The Pressure Button will allow you to simply Pressure Cook your foods using the Ninja Foodi. This will allow you to cook meals almost 70% faster than other traditional methods. Releasing the pressure naturally is often recommended for tough meats while the quick release is often suited for tender cuts like fish or even vegetables.

Air Crisp

This is possibly the most unique feature of the Ninja Foodi. Using the Air Crisp feature, you will be able to use your Ninja Foodi as an Air Fryer, that allows you to add a nice crispy and crunchy texture with little to almost no oil. This particular setting cooks the food at extremely high temperatures of 300F to 400F.

Bake/Roast

This particular function is for those who like to bake! The Bake/Roast function is an awesome mode that allows users to seamlessly use their Foodi as a regular oven (thanks to crisping lid) that allows them to create inspiring baked goods.

Steam

This particular button allows you to use the "Steam" function of the Ninja Foodi. Using steam, you will be able to cook very delicate food at high temperatures. Just make sure to use at least a cup of liquid when steaming your food. While using this feature, make sure to use the Pressure Lid.

Broil

The Broil feature is used in conjunction with the Crisping Lid in order to slightly brown or caramelizes the surface of your food. It cooks food at a higher temperature to create the required brown surface.

Slow Cooker

This particular button will allow you to utilize the Slow Cooker mode that allows you to use the Ninja Foodi as a traditional Slow Cooker. Through this method, your cooks will be cooked at a very low temperature over a prolonged period of time. The time can be adjusted from 12-4 hours, and once the cooking is done, the appliance will automatically switch to "KEEP WARM" function where the meal stays hot until you open it up.

Sear/Saute

This particular button allows you to use your Ninja Foodi to brown meat. This feature is excellent when you need searing or browning meat/ Sautéing spices. This same function can also be used to simmer sauces. Similar to Broil mode, this does not come with a temperature setting, rather, once you are done browning, you simply need to press the "START/STOP" button to initiate or stop the process.

Dehydrate

The Dehydrate function allows you to dehydrate food between 105 degrees F and 195 degrees F, and this feature will allow you to make healthy dried snacks out of meat, vegetables, and fruits. However, if you want to use this device, it is advised that you purchase a dehydrating rack for maximum efficiency.

Tips to Using Ninja Foodi

As time goes on, you will learn how to utilize the power of your Ninja Foodi to its full extent. However, the following tips will help you during the early days of your life with the Foodi and ensure that your experience is as pleasant and smooth as possible.

•   It is crucial that you don't just press the function buttons randomly! Try to read through the function of each button and use them according to the requirement of your recipe.

•   It is important that you place the lid properly while closing the appliance as it greatly affects the cooking. Therefore, make sure that your lid is tightly close by ensuring that the silicone ring inside the lid is placed all the way around the groove.

•   This is something that many people don't know, once the cooking timer of your appliance hits '0', the pot will automatically go into "Natural Pressure Release" mode where it will start to release the pressure on its own. You can use a quick release anytime to release all the steam at once, or you can wait for 10-15 minutes until the steam vents off.

•   If you are in a rush and want to release the pressure quickly, turn the pressure valve to "Open Position," which will quick release all the pressure. But this can be a little risky as a lot of steam comes out at once, so be sure to stay careful.

•   If you are dealing with a recipe that calls for unfrozen meat, make sure to use the same amount of cooking time and liquid that you would use if you were to use frozen meat of the same type.

•   Once you start using the appliance for cooking, make sure to check if the Pressure Valve is in the "Locked Position." If it is not, your appliance won't be able to build up pressure inside for cooking.

•   Make sure to keep in mind that the "Timer" button isn't a button to set time! Rather it acts as a Delay Timer. Using this button, you will be able to set a specific time, after which the Ninja Foodi will automatically wake up and start cooking the food.

Chapter 1-Breakfast Recipes

Green Beans Omelet

Prepping time: 7 minutes

Cooking time: 14 minutes

Servings: 2

Ingredients:

- 3 eggs, whisked
- 1 tablespoon cream cheese
- 1 oz green beans
- 1 teaspoon butter
- ¼ teaspoon salt
- ¼ teaspoon chili flakes

Preparation:

1. Preheat Ninja Foodi on Sauté/Stear mode.
2. Toss butter inside.
3. Add green beans and sauté them for 4 minutes.
4. Meanwhile, whisk together the eggs and cream cheese.
5. Add salt and chili flakes. Stir the liquid.
6. Pour the liquid in the pot and stir gently with the help of a spatula.
7. Lower the air fryer lid and cook an omelet for 10 minutes at 360 F.
8. Serve it!

Nutrition Values Per Serving:

calories 133, fat 10.2, fiber 0.5, carbs 1.7, protein 9

Best Asparagus Frittata

Prepping time: 10 minutes

Cooking time: 21 minutes

Servings: 2

Ingredients:

- 2 oz asparagus, chopped
- 3 eggs, whisked
- 2 tablespoons almond milk
- 1 teaspoon almond flour
- ½ teaspoon salt
- ¼ teaspoon cayenne pepper
- ½ oz Parmesan, grated
- 1 teaspoon coconut oil

Preparation:

1. Preheat the pot on "Sauté/Stear mode.
2. Add coconut oil and chopped asparagus.
3. Sauté the vegetable for 3 minutes.
4. Meanwhile, mix up together the almond milk, whisked, eggs, almond flour, cayenne pepper, and grated cheese.
5. Pour the egg mixture into the pot.
6. Close the lid and seal it.
7. Cook the frittata on High (Pressure mode) for 15 minutes.
8. After this, make a quick pressure release.
9. Lower the air fryer lid and cook the meal at 400 F for 6 minutes more.
10. When the surface of the frittata is crusty enough – finish cooking and serve it!

Nutrition Values Per Serving:

calories 165, fat 12.3, fiber 1.1, carbs 3.1, protein 11.8

Jalapeno Honey Chicken Wings

Prepping time: 15 minutes

Cooking time: 15 minutes

Servings: 4

Ingredients:

*   12 oz chicken wings
*   2 jalapeno peppers, chopped
*   1 teaspoon minced garlic
*   1 tablespoon coconut oil
*   ¼ cup of water
*   1 tablespoon butter
*   ½ teaspoon salt

Preparation:

1. Blend together the jalapeno peppers and minced garlic until smooth.
2. Then combine together the pepper mixture, salt, and coconut oil.
3. Brush every chicken wing with the pepper mixture and let for 10 minutes to marinate.
4. Place the marinated chicken wings in the pot. Add butter and water.
5. Close the lid and seal it.
6. Cook the chicken wings for 10 minutes on High 9Pressure mode).
7. Then make a quick pressure release.
8. Lower the air fryer lid and cook the chicken wings for 5 minutes more at 400 F.
9. Serve!

Nutrition Values Per Serving:

calories 220, fat 12.7, fiber 0.3, carbs 0.8, protein 24.8

Fish with Sesame

Prepping time: 8 minutes

Cooking time: 8 minutes

Servings: 4

Ingredients:

- 1.5-pound salmon fillet
- 1 tablespoon apple cider vinegar
- 1 teaspoon sesame seeds
- ¼ teaspoon dried rosemary
- ½ teaspoon salt
- 1 teaspoon butter, melted

Preparation:

1. Sprinkle the salmon fillet with the apple cider vinegar.
2. After this, mix up together the sesame seeds, dried rosemary, salt, and butter.
3. Brush the salmon with the butter sauce generously.
4. Place the salmon on the rack and lower the air fryer lid.
5. Set the air fryer mode and cook fish at 360 F for 8 minutes.
6. Serve it!

Nutrition Values Per Serving:

calories 239, fat 11.8, fiber 0.1, carbs 0.3, protein 33.1

Hard Boiled Eggs

Prepping time: 10 minutes

Cooking time: 15 minutes

Servings: 2

Ingredients:

- 4 eggs
- 1 teaspoon cream cheese
- 1 oz bacon, chopped, cooked
- 1/2 teaspoon minced garlic

Preparation:

1. Place the eggs in the air fryer basket and lower the air fryer lid.
2. Cook the eggs at 250 F for 15 minutes.
3. Meanwhile, mix up together the cooked bacon, minced garlic, and cream cheese.
4. When the eggs are cooked – chill them in ice water and peel.
5. Cut the eggs into the halves and transfer the egg yolks in the cream cheese mixture.
6. Stir it carefully until homogenous.
7. Fill the egg whites with the filling and serve!

Nutrition Values Per Serving:

calories 205, fat 15.3, fiber 0, carbs 1.2, protein 16.5

Air Crisp Cheese Casserole

Prepping time: 5 minutes

Cooking time: 22 minutes

Servings: 2

Ingredients:

- 1 oz bacon, chopped
- 2 eggs, whisked
- ¼ cup almond milk
- ½ teaspoon dried basil
- 3 oz Cheddar cheese

Preparation:

1. Mix up together the whisked eggs, almond milk and dried basil.
2. Add bacon and transfer the mixture into the springform pan.
3. Grate cheese and sprinkle it over the egg mixture.
4. Place the casserole into the Foodi and set "Air Crisp" mode 365 F.
5. Cook the casserole for 15 minutes.
6. Check the casserole and cook it for 5-7 minutes more.
7. Serve it!

Nutrition Values Per Serving:

calories 380, fat 31.5, fiber 0.7, carbs 2.8, protein 22.1

Crispy Chicken Sandwiches

Prepping time: 10 minutes

Cooking time: 15 minutes

Servings: 4

Ingredients:

- 1-pound chicken thighs, boneless, skinless
- 1 cup lettuce
- 1 teaspoon apple cider vinegar
- ½ teaspoon chili flakes
- 1 teaspoon red hot pepper
- ½ teaspoon turmeric
- 1 teaspoon white pepper
- ½ cup of water
- 1 tablespoon low-sodium soy sauce
- 1 tablespoon butter

- 1 oz Cheddar cheese, shredded

Preparation:

1. Preheat Ninja Foodi at Sauté/Stear mode for 5 minutes.
2. Toss the butter inside the pot.
3. Then rub the chicken thighs with the chili flakes, red hot pepper, turmeric, white pepper, and sprinkle with the soy sauce and apple cider vinegar.
4. Place the chicken in the pot and cook it for 5 minutes.
5. After this, close the lid and seal it.
6. Cook the chicken on High pressure for 5 minutes – quick pressure release).
7. After this, shred the chicken and remove ½ part of all the liquid from the form.
8. Lower the air fryer lid and cook the chicken at 400 F for 5 minutes more.
9. Transfer the cooked chicken on the lettuce leaves and sprinkle with cheese.
10. Taste it!

Nutrition Values Per Serving:

calories 276, fat 13.7, fiber 0.3, carbs 1.4, protein 35

Garlic Parmesan Chicken Wings

Prepping time: 10 minutes

Cooking time: 17 minutes

Servings: 2

Ingredients:

- 4 chicken wings
- ½ cup chicken stock
- ½ teaspoon salt
- 1 tablespoon butter, softened
- 1oz Parmesan, grated
- 1 teaspoon garlic powder
- 1 teaspoon minced garlic
- 1 teaspoon dried dill

Preparation:

1. Rub the chicken wings with the salt and place in the Ninja Foodi pot.
2. Add chicken stock and close the lid.
3. Seal the lid and cook chicken wings at Pressure Cook mode (High pressure) for 9 minutes.
4. Meanwhile, mix up together the butter, grated cheese, minced garlic, garlic powder, and dried dill. Whisk the mixture until homogenous.
5. When the chicken wings are cooked – make a quick pressure release. Open the lid and transfer chicken wings on the plate.
6. Remove the liquid from the pot and insert rack.
7. Brush the chicken wings with the butter mixture generously and transfer on the rack.
8. Lower the air fryer lid and press the "Broil" mode.

9. Cook the wings for 8 minutes.

10. Enjoy!

Nutrition Values Per Serving:

calories 192, fat 12.4, fiber 0.2, carbs 2.4, protein 18

Bacon Eggs Cups

Prepping time: 10 minutes

Cooking time: 15 minutes

Servings: 4

Ingredients:

- 4 eggs
- 1 tablespoon butter
- 1 teaspoon dried parsley
- ¼ teaspoon cayenne pepper
- ¼ teaspoons paprika
- 4 bacon strips
- 1 oz Parmesan, grated

Preparation:

1. Grease the small ramekins with butter.
2. Then secure the bacon strips on the edges of every ramekin.
3. Beat the egg in the center of every ramekin.
4. Sprinkle the eggs with paprika, dried parsley, cayenne pepper, and cheese.
5. Place the ramekins in the pot and lower the air fryer lid.
6. Cook the egg at 365 F for 15 minutes.
7. Chill the meal little and serve!

Nutrition Values Per Serving:

calories 212, fat 17.8, fiber 0.1, carbs 0.7, protein 11.9

Curry Shredded Chicken

Prepping time: 10 minutes

Cooking time: 35 minutes

Servings: 2

Ingredients:

- 1-pound chicken breast, skinless, boneless
- 1 teaspoon curry paste
- 2 tablespoons butter
- 1 teaspoon cayenne pepper
- ½ cup of water

Preparation:

1. Rub the chicken breast with the curry paste and place in the pot.
2. Sprinkle the poultry with cayenne pepper and add butter.
3. Pour water in the pot and close the lid. Seal the lid.
4. Set Pressure mode and cook on High for 30 minutes.
5. Then make natural pressure release for 10 minutes.
6. Open the lid and shred the chicken inside the pot with the help of the fork.
7. Then close the lid and sauté the chicken for 5 minutes more.
8. Serve it!

Nutrition Values Per Serving:

calories 380, fat 18.8, fiber 0.2, carbs 1.2, protein 48.4

Bacon Jalapeno

Prepping time: 6 minutes

Cooking time: 3 minutes

Servings: 3

Ingredients:

- 6 jalapeno peppers
- 1 teaspoon minced garlic
- 6 tablespoon cream cheese
- 6 bacon strips, chopped, cooked
- ½ teaspoon salt
- 1 oz ground beef, cooked
- ¼ teaspoon ground cumin

Preparation:

1. Trim the ends of the peppers and remove all the seeds from inside.
2. Mix up together the minced garlic, cream cheese, salt, and ground cumin. Add the ground beef and stir well. Add bacon.
3. Fill the peppers with the mixture and transfer on the rack.
4. Lower the air fryer lid and cook the jalapenos for minutes at 365 F.
5. Serve the meal immediately!

Nutrition Values Per Serving:

calories 301, fat 26, fiber 1.2, carbs 3, protein 12.9

Amazing Chili Chicken Bites

Prepping time: 7 minutes

Cooking time: 25 minutes

Servings: 3

Ingredients:

- 12 oz chicken fillet

- 1 teaspoon chili flakes
- ½ teaspoon chili pepper
- ½ teaspoon red hot pepper
- ¼ teaspoon ground cumin
- ½ teaspoon salt
- 1 tablespoon butter
- ¾ cup heavy cream

Preparation:
1. Cut the chicken fillet into the cubes.
2. Mix up together all the spices.
3. Combine together the chicken cubes and spices.
4. Then toss the butter in Ninja Foodi pot and melt it on Sauté/Stear mode.
5. Place the chicken cubes in the pot and Sauté them for 5 minutes. Stir time to time.
6. After this, add cream and stir well.
7. Lower the air fryer lid and cook the chicken bites at 360 F for 20 minutes.
8. When the time is over – serve the chicken immediately!

Nutrition Values Per Serving:

calories 354, fat 23.4, fiber 0.1, carbs 1.1, protein 33.5

Eggs in Mushroom Hats

Prepping time: 10 minutes

Cooking time: 9 minutes

Servings: 1

Ingredients:
- 4 oz mushroom hats
- 4 quail eggs
- ¼ teaspoon salt
- ½ teaspoon ground black pepper
- 1 teaspoon butter, melted

Preparation:
1. Spread the mushroom hats with the butter inside.
2. Then beat the eggs into the mushroom hats and sprinkle with the ground black pepper and salt.
3. Transfer the mushroom hats on the rack and lower the air fryer lid.
4. Cook the meal at 365 F for 7 minutes.
5. Then check the mushrooms and cook them for 2 minutes more.
6. Serve it!

Nutrition Values Per Serving:

calories 118, fat 8.2, fiber 1., carbs 4.6, protein 8.4

Classical Fried Eggs

Prepping time: 5 minutes

Cooking time: 10 minutes

Servings: 2

Ingredients:

- 4 eggs
- 1 teaspoon butter
- ¼ teaspoon ground black pepper
- ¾ teaspoon salt

Preparation:

1. Grease the small egg pan with the butter.
2. Beat the eggs in the egg pan and sprinkle with the ground black pepper and salt.
3. Transfer the egg pan in the pot and lower the air fryer lid.
4. Cook the eggs for 10 minutes at 350 F.
5. Serve the cooked eggs immediately!

Nutrition Values Per Serving:

calories 143, fat 10.7, fiber 0.1, carbs 0.9, protein 11.1

Feta Frittata

Prepping time: 10 minutes

Cooking time: 15 minutes

Servings: 3

Ingredients:

- 4 oz fresh spinach, chopped
- 3 eggs, beaten
- 1 oz Feta, crumbled
- ¼ teaspoon white pepper
- ¼ teaspoon salt

Preparation:

1. Whisk the eggs well.
2. Stir the spinach in the whisked eggs and add white pepper and salt.
3. After this, add Feta cheese and mix up the egg mixture with the help of the spoon gently
4. Transfer the liquid in the springform pan.
5. Insert the air fryer rack in Ninja Foodi and place the frittata.
6. Lower the air fryer lid and cook frittata at 360 F.
7. Cook for 15 minutes or until the meal is set. Serve it!

Nutrition Values Per Serving:

calories 97, fat 6.5, fiber 0.9, carbs 2.2, protein 8

Keto Cheddar Bites

Prepping time: 6 minutes

Cooking time: 12 minutes

Servings: 4

Ingredients:

- 4 eggs
- ¼ cup heavy cream
- 3 oz Cheddar cheese, shredded
- 3 oz shrimps, peeled, cooked
- ½ teaspoon salt
- ½ cup of water

Preparation:

1. Beat the eggs in the bowl and whisk well.
2. Add heavy cream, salt, and cheese. Stir it.
3. Chop the shrimps roughly and add in egg mixture.
4. Pour the egg mixture into the muffin molds.
5. Add water in the pot.
6. Place the muffins molds on the rack.
7. Cover the molds with the foil well.
8. Close the lid and seal it.
9. Cook the bites on High for 12 minutes. (Natural pressure release)
10. Discard the foil from bites and transfer them on the serving plates. Taste it!

Nutrition Values Per Serving:

calories 200, fat 14.6, fiber 0, carbs 1.1, protein 15.8

Breakfast Pork Chops

Prepping time: 10 minutes

Cooking time: 30 minutes

Servings: 2

Ingredients:

- 2 pork chops
- 1 teaspoon butter
- ½ teaspoon dried cilantro
- 1 oz Mozzarella, sliced
- ½ teaspoon cayenne pepper
- ¾ cup of water

Preparation:

1. Sprinkle the pork chops with the dried cilantro and cayenne pepper.

2. Toss the butter in Foodi and melt it on Sauté/Stear mode.
3. Add pork chops and cook them for 2 minutes from each side.
4. Add water and close the lid.
5. Cook the meat on "Sauté/Stear" mode for 25 minutes.
6. When the pork chops are cooked – open the lid and cover the meat with the sliced cheese.
7. Lower the air fryer lid and cook the meat for 3 minutes more at 400 F.
8. Enjoy!

Nutrition Values Per Serving:

calories 314, fat 24.4, fiber 0.1, carbs 0.8, protein 22.1

Keto Juicy Bacon Strips

Prepping time: 5 minutes

Cooking time: 7 minutes

Servings: 2

Ingredients:

- 10 bacon strips
- ¼ teaspoon dried basil
- ¼ teaspoon chili flakes
- 1/3 teaspoon salt

Preparation:

1. Rub the bacon strips with the dried basil, chili flakes, and salt.
2. Place the bacon on the rack and lower the air fryer lid.
3. Cook the bacon for 5 minutes at 400 F.
4. Check if the bacon is cooked and cook for 3 minutes more or until you get the desired doneness.

Nutrition Values Per Serving:

calories 500, fat 45, fiber 0, carbs 0, protein 20

Quiche Lorraine

Prepping time: 10 minutes

Cooking time: 15 minutes

Servings: 4

Ingredients:

- 4 eggs, whisked
- ½ teaspoon salt
- ½ teaspoon cayenne pepper
- ¼ cup heavy cream
- 2 oz bacon, chopped
- 1 tablespoon butter
- 3oz Parmesan, grated

- ½ teaspoon dried basil

Preparation:

1. Preheat Ninja Foodi at "Sauté/Stear" mode for 5 minutes.
2. Then add butter and melt it.
3. Add bacon and sauté it for 4 minutes.
4. Meanwhile, whisk together the eggs, salt, cayenne pepper, dried basil, and heavy cream.
5. When the bacon is cooked – add the egg mixture and lower the air fryer lid.
6. Cook the meal for 10 minutes at 365 F.
7. Then top the egg mixture with the grated cheese and cook for 5 minutes more.
8. Serve it!

Nutrition Values Per Serving:

calories 260, fat 20.5, fiber 0.1, carbs 1.6, protein 17.8

Asparagus and Bacon Plate

Prepping time: 6 minutes

Cooking time: 9 minutes

Servings: 2

Ingredients:

- 2 oz bacon, chopped
- 4 oz asparagus, chopped
- ½ teaspoon salt
- ½ teaspoon ground black pepper
- 1 tablespoon butter
- 1 cup water, for cooking

Preparation:

1. Place the bacon on the air fryer rack and sprinkle with the ground black pepper.
2. Lower the air fryer lid and cook the bacon at 400 F for 8 minutes.
3. Flip the bacon into another side after 4 minutes of cooking.
4. Then transfer the cooked bacon on the plate.
5. Pour water in the pot and insert steamer rack.
6. Place the asparagus and close the lid.
7. Cook the asparagus on High for 5 minutes. Then make quick pressure release.
8. Transfer the cooked asparagus over the bacon.
9. Add butter and salt.
10. Serve it!

Nutrition Values Per Serving:

calories 217, fat 17.7, fiber 1.3, carbs 3, protein 11.9

Chorizo Fritatta

Prepping time: 10 minutes

Cooking time: 20 minutes

Servings: 6

Ingredients:

- 5 eggs, whisked
- 1 oz fresh parsley, chopped
- 3 oz chorizo, chopped
- 1 teaspoon salt
- ¼ green pepper, chopped
- 1 teaspoon butter
- ¼ cup heavy cream
- 1 oz broccoli, chopped
- 1 oz Cheddar cheese, grated
- 1 teaspoon cream cheese
- 1 teaspoon paprika
- 1 cup of water (for cooking on High pressure)

Preparation:

1. Grease the springform pan with the butter.
2. Then place the layer of green pepper and broccoli.
3. After this, whisk together eggs, parsley, salt, heavy cream, cream cheese, and paprika.
4. Add chorizo and cheese. Stir gently and transfer the mixture in the pan. Flatten it gently.
5. Pour water in the pan and place the springform cake on the rack.
6. Close the lid and seal it.
7. Cook the meal on High (Pressure mode) for 20 minutes. Then use the quick pressure release method for 5 minutes.
8. Serve it!

Nutrition Values Per Serving:

calories 166, fat 13.4, fiber 0.5, carbs 1.8, protein 9.7

Butter Chicken Bites

Prepping time: 10 minutes

Cooking time: 11 minutes

Servings: 3

Ingredients:

- 10 oz chicken thighs, boneless, skinless
- 1 teaspoon turmeric
- 1 teaspoon chili flakes
- ½ teaspoon salt

- ¼ teaspoon ground nutmeg
- ¾ teaspoon ground ginger
- ½ cup heavy cream
- 2 tablespoon butter
- 1 teaspoon kosher salt

Preparation:

1. Preheat Ninja Foodi pot at Sauté /Stear mode for 5 minutes.
2. Toss the butter in the pot and melt it.
3. Add turmeric, chili flakes, salt, and ground nutmeg. Then, add ground ginger and salt.
4. Bring to boil the mixture.
5. Meanwhile, chop the chicken thighs roughly.
6. Transfer the chicken thighs in the pot and cooks for 5 minutes at Sauté mode.
7. After this, add heavy cream and close the lid. Seal the lid.
8. Select Pressure mode and set High pressure
9. Cook it for 6 minutes. Then make a quick pressure release.
10. Chill the cooked chicken bites little and serve!

Nutrition Values Per Serving:

calories 322, fat 22.3, fiber 0.3, carbs 1.5, protein 28

Western Omelet

Prepping time: 5 minutes

Cooking time: 34 minutes

Servings: 2

Ingredients:
- 3 eggs, whisked
- 5 tablespoon almond milk
- 3 oz chorizo, chopped
- 1 green pepper, chopped
- ¼ teaspoon salt
- ¾ teaspoon chili flakes
- 1 oz Feta cheese, crumbled

Preparation:

1. Mix up together all the ingredients and stir gently.
2. Pour the mixture into the omelet pan.
3. Preheat Ninja Foodi at "Roast/Bake" mode at 320 F for 4 minutes.
4. Then transfer the pan with an omelet in Ninja Foodi and cook at the same mode for 30 minutes.
5. Serve the cooked meal hot!

Nutrition Values Per Serving:

calories 424, fat 34.9, fiber 1.9, carbs 6.8, protein 21.9

Breakfast Muffins

Prepping time: 10 minutes

Cooking time: 15 minutes

Servings: 2

Ingredients:

- 1 tablespoon cream cheese
- 1 teaspoon butter
- 1 egg, beaten
- 1 tablespoon almond flour
- 2 oz Cheddar cheese, grated
- ¼ teaspoon ground black pepper
- ½ teaspoon salt
- ½ teaspoon paprika
- ½ cup water (for cooking on High)

Preparation:

1. Mix up together the cream cheese, butter, egg, almond flour, cheese, ground black pepper, salt, and paprika.
2. Whisk the mixture until smooth.
3. After this, pour ½ cup of water in the pot. Insert the rack.
4. Transfer the batter in the prepared muffins molds and place on the rack.
5. Cover the muffins with the foil and close the lid.
6. Make sure you seal the lid and cook on PRESSURE mode (High) for 15 minutes.
7. Then make the quick pressure release for 5 minutes.
8. Chill the muffins little and serve!

Nutrition Values Per Serving:

calories 203, fat 17, fiber 0.7, carbs 1.9, protein 11.1

Low Carb Morning Casserole

Prepping time: 5 minutes

Cooking time: 10 minutes

Servings: 3

Ingredients:

- 3 oz cauliflower hash brown, cooked
- 3 eggs, whisked
- ¾ cup almond milk
- 2 oz chorizo, chopped
- 1 oz mozzarella, sliced
- 1/3 teaspoon chili flakes
- ½ teaspoon butter

Preparation:

1. Melt the butter and whisk it together with the chili flakes, chorizo, almond milk, and eggs.

2. Add hash brown and stir gently.

3. Place the egg mixture in the cake pan and place in the Ninja Foodi.

4. Cook on Air Crisp 365 F for 8 minutes.

5. Then add sliced mozzarella on the top and cook for 2 minutes more, or until you get the desired doneness.

6. Enjoy!

Nutrition Values Per Serving:

calories 326, fat 28.2, fiber 1.9, carbs 5.8, protein 14.7

Chapter 2-Snacks and Appetizers Recipes

Cauliflower and Egg Dish

Prepping time: 10 minutes

Cooking time: 4 minutes

Servings: 4

Ingredients:

- 21 ounces cauliflower, separated into florets
- 1 cup red onion, chopped
- 1 cup celery, chopped
- ½ cup of water
- Salt and pepper to taste
- 2 tablespoons balsamic vinegar
- 1 teaspoon stevia
- 4 boiled eggs, chopped
- 1 cup Keto Friendly mayonnaise

Preparation:

1. Add water to Ninja Foodi
2. Add steamer basket and add cauliflower, lock lid and cook on High Pressure for 5 minutes
3. Quick release pressure. Transfer cauliflower to bowl and add eggs, celery, onion and toss
4. Take another bowl and mix in mayo, salt, pepper, vinegar, stevia and whisk well
5. Add a salad, toss well. Divide into salad bowls and serve. Enjoy!

Nutrition Values Per Serving:

Calories: 170, Fat: 4g, Carbohydrates: 5g, Protein: 5g

Ultimate Cheese Dredged Cauliflower Snack

Prepping time: 10 minutes

Cooking time: 30 minutes

Servings: 4

Ingredients:

- 1 tablespoon mustard
- 1 head cauliflower
- 1 teaspoon avocado mayonnaise
- ½ cup parmesan cheese, grated
- ¼ cup butter, cut into small pieces

Preparation:

1. Set your Ninja Foodi to Saute mode and add butter and cauliflower
2. Saute for 3 minutes. Add remaining ingredients and stir

3. Lock lid and cook on HIGH pressure for 30 minutes. Release pressure naturally over 10 minutes

4. Serve and enjoy!

Nutrition Values Per Serving:

Calories: 155, Fat: 13g, Carbohydrates: 4g, Protein: 6g

Obvious Cabbage and Paprika

Prepping time: 10 minutes

Cooking time: 4 minutes

Servings: 4

Ingredients:

- 1 and ½ pounds green cabbage, shredded
- Salt and pepper to taste
- 3 tablespoon ghee
- 1 cup vegetable stock
- ¼ teaspoon sweet paprika

Preparation:

1. Set your Ninja Foodi to Saute mode and add ghee, let it melt
2. Add cabbage, salt, pepper, and stock, stir well
3. Lock lid and cook on HIGH pressure for 7 minutes. Quick release pressure
4. Add paprika and toss well. Divide between plates and serve. Enjoy!

Nutrition Values Per Serving:

Calories: 170, Fat: 4g, Carbohydrates: 5g, Protein: 5g

Inspiring Cauliflower Hash Browns

Prepping time: 10 minutes

Cooking time: 30 minutes

Servings: 6

Ingredients:

- 6 whole eggs
- 4 cups cauliflower rice
- ¼ cup milk
- 1 onion, chopped
- 3 tablespoons butter
- 1 and ½ cups cooked ham, chopped
- ½ cup shredded cheese

Preparation:

1. Set your Ninja Foodi to sauté mode and add butter, let the butter heat up
2. Add onions and cook for 5 minutes until tender. Add iced cauliflower to pot and stir

3. Lock the Air Crisping lid and Air Crisp for 15 minutes, making sure to give them a turn about halfway through

4. Take a small bowl and mix in eggs and milk, pour mixture over browned cauliflower

5. Sprinkle ham over top. Press Air Crispy again and crisp for 10 minutes more

6. Sprinkle cheddar cheese on top and lock lid, let the crisp for 1 minute more until the cheese melts. Serve and enjoy!

Nutrition Values Per Serving:

Calories: 166, Fat: 14g, Carbohydrates: 3g, Protein: 9g

Almonds and Kale Mix

Prepping time: 10 minutes

Cooking time: 4 minutes

Servings: 4

Ingredients:

- 1 cup of water
- 1 big kale bunch, chopped
- 1 tablespoon balsamic vinegar
- 1/3 cup toasted almonds
- 3 garlic cloves, minced
- 1 small yellow onion, chopped
- 2 tablespoons olive oil

Preparation:

1. Set your Ninja Foodi on Saute mode and add oil, let it heat up

2. Stir in onion and cook for 3 minutes. Add garlic, water, kale, and stir

3. Lock lid and cook on HIGH pressure for 4 minutes. Quick release pressure

4. Add salt, pepper, vinegar, almonds and toss well. Serve and enjoy!

Nutrition Values Per Serving:

Calories: 140, Fat: 6g, Carbohydrates: 5g, Protein: 3g

Veggies Dredged in Cheese

Prepping time: 10 minutes

Cooking time: 30 minutes

Servings: 4

Ingredients:

- 2 onions, sliced
- 2 tomatoes, sliced
- 2 zucchinis, sliced
- 2 teaspoons olive oil
- 2 cups cheddar cheese, grated

- 2 teaspoons mixed dried herbs
- Salt and pepper to taste

Preparation:

Arrange all the listed ingredients to your Ninja Foodi. Top with olive oil, herbs, cheddar, salt and pepper. Lock lid and Air Crisp for 30 minutes at 350 degrees F. Serve and enjoy!

Nutrition Values Per Serving:

Calories: 305, Fat: 22g, Carbohydrates: 9g, Protein: 15g

Authentic Western Omelet

Prepping time: 5 minutes

Cooking time: 34 minutes

Serving: 2

Ingredients:
- 3 eggs, whisked
- 3 ounces chorizo, chopped
- 1-ounces Feta cheese, crumbled
- 5 tablespoons almond milk
- ¾ teaspoon chili flakes
- ¼ teaspoon salt
- 1 green pepper, chopped

Preparation:

1. Add all the ingredients and mix them well. Stir it gently. Take an omelet pan and pour the mixture into it. Preheat your Ninja Foodi at "Roast/Bake" mode at 320 F.
2. Cook for 4 minutes. After that, transfer the pan with an omelet in Ninja Foodi
3. Cook for 30 minutes more at the same mode. Serve hot and enjoy!

Nutrition Values Per Serving:

Calories: 426, Fat: 38.2g, Carbohydrates: 6.8g, Protein: 21.7g

Bite Zucchini Fries

Prepping time: 10 minutes

Cooking time: 10 minutes

Servings: 4

Ingredients:
- 1-2 pounds of zucchini, sliced into 2 and ½ inch sticks
- Salt to taste
- 1 cup cream cheese
- 2 tablespoons olive oil

Preparation:

1. Add zucchini in a colander and season with salt, add cream cheese and mix

2. Add oil into your Ninja Foodi's pot and add Zucchini

3. Lock Air Crisping Lid and set the temperature to 365 degrees F and timer to 10 minutes

4. Let it cook for 10 minutes and take the dish out once done, enjoy!

Nutrition Values Per Serving:

Calories: 374, Fat: 36g, Carbohydrates: 6g, Protein: 7g

Green Chili Pickle Recipe

Prepping time: 5 minutes

Cooking time: 11 minutes

Servings: 4

Ingredients:

- 1 pound green chilies
- 1 and ½ cups apple cider vinegar
- 1 teaspoon pickling salt
- 1 and ½ teaspoon sugar
- ¼ teaspoon garlic powder

Preparation:

1. Add the listed ingredients to your pot. Lock up the lid and cook on HIGH pressure for 11 minutes. Release the pressure naturally

2. Spoon the mixture into jars and cover the slices with cooking liquid, making sure to completely submerge the chilies. Serve!

Nutrition Values Per Serving:

Calories: 3, Fat: 0g, Carbohydrates: 0.8g, Protein: 0.1g

Garlic Chicken Livers

Prepping time: 10 minutes

Cooking time: 8 hours

Serving: 6

Ingredients:

- 1 pound chicken livers
- 8 garlic cloves, minced
- 8 ounces cremini mushrooms, quartered
- 4 slices uncooked bacon, chopped
- 1 onion, chopped
- 1 cup bone broth
- 1 teaspoon dried thyme
- 1 teaspoon dried rosemary
- 1 teaspoon salt
- 1 teaspoon freshly ground black pepper

- ¼ cup fresh parsley, chopped

Preparation:

1. Add livers, bacon, garlic, mushrooms, onion, thyme, broth, rosemary to Ninja Foodi
2. Season with salt and pepper. Place lid and cook on SLOW COOK Mode (LOW) for 8 hours
3. Remove lid and stir in parsley. Serve and enjoy!

Nutrition Values Per Serving:

Calories: 210, Fat: 9g, Carbohydrates: 6g, Protein: 24g

The Zucchini Gratin

Prepping time: 10 minutes

Cooking time: 15 minutes

Servings: 4

Ingredients:

- 2 zucchinis
- 1 tablespoon fresh parsley, chopped
- 2 tablespoons bread crumbs
- 4 tablespoons parmesan cheese, grated
- 1 tablespoon vegetable oil
- Salt and pepper to taste

Preparation:

1. Pre-heat your Ninja Foodi to 300 degrees F for 3 minutes
2. Slice zucchini lengthwise to get about 8 equal sizes pieces
3. Arrange pieces in your Crisping Basket (skin side down)
4. Top each with parsley, bread crumbs, cheese, oil, salt, and pepper
5. Return basket Ninja Foodi basket and cook for 15 minutes at 360 degrees F
6. Once done, serve with sauce. Enjoy!

Nutrition Values Per Serving:

Calories: 481, Fat: 11g, Carbohydrates: 10g, Protein: 7g

Baked Egg Frittata

Prepping time: 10 minutes

Cooking time: 15 minutes

Servings: 4

Ingredients:

- 5 whole eggs
- ¾ teaspoon mixed herbs
- 1 cup spinach
- ¼ cup shredded cheddar cheese
- ½ cup mushrooms

- Salt and pepper to taste
- ¾ cup half and half
- 2 tablespoons butter

Preparation:

1. Dice mushrooms, chop spinach finely
2. Set your Ninja Foodi to Saute mode and add spinach, mushrooms
3. Whisk eggs, milk, cream cheese, herbs, and Sautéed vegetables in a bowl and mix well
4. Take a 6-inch baking pan and grease it well
5. Pour mixture and transfer to your Ninja Foodi (on a trivet)
6. Cook on HIGH pressure for 2 minutes. Quick release pressure. Serve and enjoy!

Nutrition Values Per Serving:

Calories: 300, Fat: 25g, Carbohydrates: 5g, Protein: 14g

Rise and Shine Casserole

Prepping time: 10 minutes

Cooking time: 10 minutes

Serving: 6

Ingredients:

- 4 whole eggs
- 1 tablespoons milk
- 1 cup ham, cooked and chopped
- ½ cup cheddar cheese, shredded
- ¼ teaspoon salt
- ¼ teaspoon ground black pepper

Preparation:

1. Take a baking pan (small enough to fit into your Ninja Foodi) bowl, and grease it well with butter. Take a medium bowl and whisk in eggs, milk, salt, pepper and add ham, cheese, and stir. Pour mixture into baking pan and lower the pan into your Ninja Foodi

2. Set your Ninja Foodi Air Crisp mode and Air Crisp for 325 degrees F for 7 minutes

3. Remove pan from eggs and enjoy!

Nutrition Values Per Serving:

Calories: 169, Fat: 13g, Carbohydrates: 1g, Protein: 12g

Quick Turkey Cutlets

Prepping time: 10 minutes

Cooking time: 22 minutes

Servings: 4

Ingredients:

- 1 teaspoon Greek seasoning

- 1 pound turkey cutlets
- 2 tablespoons olive oil
- 1 teaspoon turmeric powder
- ½ cup almond flour

Preparation:

1. Add Greek seasoning, turmeric powder, almond flour to a bowl
2. Dredge turkey cutlets in it and keep it on the side for 30 minutes
3. Set your Foodi to Saute mode and add oil and cutlets, Saute for 2 minutes
4. Lock lid and cook on LOW-MEDIUM pressure for 20 minutes
5. Quick release pressure. Serve and enjoy!

Nutrition Values Per Serving:

Calories: 233, Fat: 19g, Carbohydrates: 3.7g, Protein: 36g

Everybody's Favorite Cauliflower Patties

Prepping time: 5 minutes

Cooking time: 20 minutes

Servings: 4

Ingredients:

- 3 whole eggs
- 1 chili pepper, chopped
- ½ teaspoon garlic powder
- Salt and pepper to taste
- 2 cups cauliflower, chopped
- ¾ cups olive oil
- ¼ cup cheddar cheese
- ¼ cup whole mozzarella cheese

Preparation:

1. Cut cauliflower into small florets, remove leaves and cut out a core
2. Add 1 cup water to Ninja Food, transfer florets to steamer basket and place it on a trivet in your Ninja Foodi. Lock lid and cook on HIGH pressure for 5 minutes
3. Mash steamed cauliflower and dry them, add shredded cheese, eggs, chili, salt and pepper
4. Mix well and shape into flat patties
5. Heat up oil in your Ninja Foodi and set to Saute mode, shallow fry patties until crisp on both sides. Serve and enjoy!

Nutrition Values Per Serving:

Calories: 550, Fat: 54g, Carbohydrates: 5g, Protein: 13g

Bowl Full of Broccoli Salad

Prepping time: 10 minutes

Cooking time: 5 minutes

Servings: 4

Ingredients:

- 1 pound broccoli, cut into florets
- 2 tablespoons balsamic vinegar
- 2 garlic cloves, minced
- 1 teaspoon mustard seeds
- 1 teaspoon cumin seeds
- Salt and pepper to taste
- 1 cup cottage cheese, crumbled

Preparation:

1. Add 1 cup water to your Ninja Foodi. Place steamer basket
2. Place broccoli in basket and lock lid, cook on HIGH pressure for 5 minutes
3. Quick release pressure and remove lid. Toss broccoli with other ingredients and serve. Enjoy!

Nutrition Values Per Serving:

Calories: 95, Fat: 3.1g, Carbohydrates: 10g, Protein: 2g

Baked Egg Dredged Casserole

Prepping time: 10 minutes

Cooking time: 5 minutes

Serving: 6

Ingredients:

- 4 whole eggs
- 1 tablespoons milk
- 1 tomato, diced
- ½ cup spinach
- ¼ teaspoon salt
- ¼ teaspoon ground black pepper

Preparation:

1. Take a baking pan (small enough to fit Ninja Foodi) and grease it with butter
2. Take a medium bowl and whisk in eggs, milk, salt, pepper, add veggies to the bowl and stir
3. Pour egg mixture into the baking pan and lower the pan into the Ninja Foodi
4. Close Air Crisping lid and Air Crisp for 325 degrees for 7 minutes
5. Remove the pan from eggs and enjoy hot!

Nutrition Values Per Serving:

Calories: 78, Fat: 5g, Carbohydrates: 1g, Protein: 7g

Spaghetti Squash and Chicken Parmesan

Prepping time: 10 minutes

Cooking time: 20 minutes

Servings: 4

Ingredients:

- 1 spaghetti squash
- 1 cup marinara sauce (Keto Friendly)
- 1 pound chicken, cooked and cubed
- 16 ounces mozzarella

Preparation:

1. Split up the squash in halves and remove the seeds
2. Add 1 cup of water to the Ninja Foodi and place a trivet on top
3. Add the squash halves on the trivet. Lock up the lid and cook for 20 minutes at HIGH pressure
4. Do a quick release. Remove the squashes and shred them using a fork into spaghetti portions
5. Pour sauce over the squash and give it a nice mix
6. Top them up with the cubed up chicken and top with mozzarella
7. Broil for 1-2 minutes and broil until the cheese has melted

Nutrition Values Per Serving:

Calories: 127, Fats: 8g, Carbs:11g, Protein:5g

Simple Treat of Garlic

Prepping time: 10 minutes

Cooking time: 5 minutes

Servings: 4

Ingredients:

- 1 tablespoon extra-virgin olive oil
- 2 garlic cloves, minced
- 2 large-sized Belgian endive, halved lengthwise
- ½ cup apple cider vinegar
- ½ cup broth
- Salt and pepper to taste
- 1 teaspoon cayenne pepper

Preparation:

1. Set your Ninja Foodi to Saute mode and add oil, let the oil heat up
2. Add garlic and cook for 30 seconds unto browned
3. Add endive, vinegar, broth, salt, pepper, and cayenne
4. Lock lid and cook on LOW pressure for 2 minutes. Quick release pressure and serve. Enjoy!

Nutrition Values Per Serving:

Calories: 91, Fat: 6g, Carbohydrates: 3g, Protein: 2g

Excellent Bacon and Cheddar Frittata

Prepping time: 10 minutes

Cooking time: 10 minutes

Serving: 6

Ingredients:

- 6 whole eggs
- 2 tablespoons milk
- ½ cup bacon, cooked and chopped
- 1 cup broccoli, cooked
- ½ cup shredded cheddar cheese
- ¼ teaspoon salt
- ¼ teaspoon ground black pepper

Preparation:

1. Take a baking pan (small enough to fit into your Ninja Foodi) bowl, and grease it well with butter. Take a medium sized bowl and add eggs, milk, salt, pepper, bacon, broccoli, and cheese. Stir well. Pour mixture into your prepared baking pan and lower pan into your Foodi, close Air Crisping lid. Air Crisp for 7 minutes at 375 degrees F. Remove pan and enjoy!

Nutrition Values Per Serving:

Calories: 269, Fat: 20g, Carbohydrates: 3g, Protein: 19g

Pork Packed Jalapeno

Prepping time: 10 minutes

Cooking time: 10 minutes

Serving: 6

Ingredients:

- 2 pounds pork sausage, ground
- 2 cups parmesan cheese, shredded
- 2 pounds large sized jalapeno peppers sliced lengthwise and seeded
- 2 (8 ounces packages), cream cheese, softened
- 2 (8 ounces) bottles, ranch dressing

Preparation:

1. Take a bowl and add pork sausage, cream cheese, ranch dressing and mix well
2. Slice jalapeno in half, remove seeds and clean them
3. Stuff sliced jalapeno pieces with pork mixture
4. Place peppers in crisping basket and transfer basket to your Ninja Foodi
5. Lock Air Crisping lid and cook on Air Crisp mode for 10 minutes at 350 degrees F
6. Cook in batches if needed, serve and enjoy!

Nutrition Values Per Serving:

Calories: 609, Fat: 50g, Carbohydrates: 10g, Protein: 29g

The Great Mediterranean Spinach

Prepping time: 10 minutes

Cooking time: 15 minutes

Servings: 4

Ingredients:

- 4 tablespoons butter
- 2 pounds spinach, chopped and boiled
- Salt and pepper to taste
- 2/3 cup Kalamata olives, halved and pitted
- 1 and ½ cups feta cheese, grated
- 4 teaspoons fresh lemon zest, grated

Preparation:

1. Take a bowl and mix in spinach, butter, salt, pepper and mix well
2. Transfer to Ninja Foodi the seasoned spinach
3. Lock Air Crisper and Air Crisp for 15 minutes at 350 degrees F. Serve and enjoy!

Nutrition Values Per Serving:

Calories: 247, Fat: 13g, Carbohydrates: 4g, Protein: 6g

Buttered Up Garlic and Fennel

Prepping time: 10 minutes, Cooking time: 5 minutes

Servings: 4

Ingredients:

- ½ stick butter
- 2 garlic cloves, sliced
- ½ teaspoon salt
- 1 and ½ pounds fennel bulbs, cut into wedges
- ¼ teaspoon ground black pepper
- ½ teaspoon cayenne
- ¼ teaspoon dried dill weed
- 1/3 cup dry white wine
- 2/3 cup stock

Preparation:

1. Set your Ninja Foodi to Saute mode and add butter, let it heat up
2. Add garlic and cook for 30 seconds. Add rest of the ingredients
3. Lock lid and cook on LOW pressure for 3 minutes. Remove lid and serve. Enjoy!

Nutrition Values Per Serving:

Calories: 111, Fat: 6g, Carbohydrates: 2g, Protein: 2g

Chapter 3-Beef, Pork and Lamb Recipes

Stuffed Pork Roll

Prepping Time: 20 minutes

Cooking time: 15 minutes

Servings: 4

Ingredients:

- 1 scallion, chopped
- ¼ cup sun-dried tomatoes, chopped finely
- 2 tablespoons fresh parsley, chopped
- Salt and ground black pepper, as required
- 4 (6-ounce pork cutlets, pounded slightly
- 2 teaspoons paprika
- ½ tablespoon olive oil

Preparation:

In a bowl, mix together, scallion, tomatoes, parsley, salt and black pepper. Coat each cutlet with tomato mixture. Roll each cutlet and secure with cocktail sticks. Rub the outer part of rolls with paprika, salt and black pepper. Coat the rolls with oil evenly. Arrange the greased "Cook & Crisp Basket" in the pot of Ninja Foodi. Close the Ninja Foodi with crisping lid and select "Air Crisp". Set the temperature to 390 degrees F for 5 minutes. Press "Start/Stop" to begin preheating. After preheating, open the lid. Place the rolls into the "Cook & Crisp Basket". Close the Ninja Foodi with crisping lid and select "Air Crisp". Set the temperature to 390 degrees F for 15minutes.

Press "Start/Stop" to begin cooking.

Nutrition Values Per Serving:

Calories: 224 Fats: 8.4g Net Carbs: 0.9g Carbs: 1.6g Fiber: 0.7g Sugar: 0.5g Proteins: 36.1g Sodium: 41mg

Pulled Pork

Prepping Time: 15 minutes

Cooking time: 38 minutes

Servings: 6

Ingredients:

- 2 pounds boneless pork shoulder, cut into 1-inch cubes
- 3 tablespoons fresh lemon juice
- 6 garlic cloves, crushed
- 2 teaspoons fresh lemon zest, grated
- 1 teaspoon dried oregano
- 1½ teaspoons red chili powder
- 1 teaspoon ground cumin

- Salt and ground black pepper, as required
- ½ large onion, peeled
- ½ cup homemade chicken broth

Preparation:

In the pot of Ninja Foodi, place the pork shoulder, lemon juice, garlic, lemon zest, oregano, chili powder, cumin, salt and black pepper and stir to combine. Top with the onion and broth. Close the Ninja Foodi with pressure lid and place the pressure valve to "Seal" position. Select "Pressure" and set to "High" for 20 minutes. Press "Start/Stop" to begin cooking. Switch the valve to "Vent" and do a "Quick" release. Remove the onion from the pot and shred the meat. Select "Sauté/Sear" setting of Ninja Foodi and press "Start/Stop" to begin cooking. Cook for about 15 minutes, stirring occasionally. Press "Start/Stop" to stop cooking.

Serve hot.

Nutrition Values Per Serving:

Calories: 236 Fats: 5.7g Net Carbs: 2.5g Carbs: 3.3g Fiber: 0.8g Sugar: 0.9g Proteins: 40.6g Sodium: 187mg

Honey Glazed Ham

Prepping Time: 15 minutes

Cooking time: 40 minutes

Servings: 4

Ingredients:

- 1 pound 10½ ounces sugar-free ham
- 1 cup homemade chicken broth
- 2 tablespoons French mustard
- 1 tablespoon yacon syrup

Preparation:

1. Place the ham at room temperature for about 30 minutes before cooking.
2. In a bowl, mix together the whiskey, mustard, and yacon syrup.
3. Place the ham in a baking pan with half of the yacon syrup mixture and coat well.
4. Arrange the "Cook & Crisp Basket" in the pot of Ninja Foodi.
5. Close the Ninja Foodi with crisping lid and select "Air Crisp".
6. Set the temperature to 320 degrees F for 5 minutes.
7. Press "Start/Stop" to begin preheating.
8. After preheating, open the lid.
9. Place the baking pan into the "Cook & Crisp Basket".
10. Close the Ninja Foodi with crisping lid and select "Air Crisp".
11. Set the temperature to 320 degrees F for 40 minutes.
12. Press "Start/Stop" to begin cooking.
13. After 15 minutes of cooking, flip the side of ham and top with the remaining yacon syrup mixture.

14. Place the ham onto a platter for about 10 minutes before slicing.

15. Cut into desired size slices and serve.

Nutrition Values Per Serving:

Calories: 279 Fats: 14.5g Net Carbs: 6.1g Carbs: 8.7g Fiber: 2.6g Sugar: 1.1g Proteins: 27g Sodium: 2113mg

Pork & Bacon Meatballs in Tomato Sauce

Prepping Time: 20 minutes

Cooking time: 11 minutes

Servings: 4

Ingredients:

For Meatballs:

- 1½ pounds lean ground pork
- 6 slices bacon
- 1 organic egg
- ½ of small onion, chopped
- 2 teaspoons garlic, minced
- ½ tablespoon fresh parsley, chopped
- 1 teaspoon low-sodium soy sauces
- Salt and ground black pepper, as required

For Sauce:

- Olive oil cooking spray
- 4 cups canned tomatoes, pureed
- ½ tablespoon Italian seasoning
- 1 teaspoon onion powder
- 1 teaspoon garlic salt
- Salt and ground black pepper, as required
- 2 bay leaves
- ½ cup water

Preparation:

1. For meatballs: in a food processor, add all ingredients and pulse until well combined.
2. Make small equal-sized balls from the mixture.
3. Select "Sauté/Sear" setting of Ninja Foodi and grease the pot with cooking spray generously.
4. Press "Start/Stop" to begin cooking and heat for about 2-3 minutes.
5. Add all the sauce ingredients except the water and cook for about 2-3 minutes.
6. Press "Start/Stop" to begin cooking and place the meatballs in sauce.
7. Pour water on top.
8. Close the Ninja Foodi with the pressure lid and place the pressure valve to "Seal" position.
9. Select "Pressure" and set to "High for 8 minutes.
10. Press "Start/Stop" to begin cooking.

11. Switch the valve to "Vent" and do a "Natural" release.

12. Serve hot.

Nutrition Values Per Serving:

Calories: 517 Fats: 36.6g Net Carbs: 5.9g Carbs: 8g Fiber: 2.1g Sugar: 4g Proteins: 38.8g Sodium: 860mg

Zesty Pork Meatballs

Prepping Time: 15 minutes

Cooking time: 5 minutes

Servings: 8

Ingredients:

For Meatballs:

- 1½ pounds ground pork
- 2 tablespoons fresh ginger, grated
- 1 tablespoon garlic, minced
- 1 tablespoon lemongrass paste
- 1 teaspoon fresh lime zest, grated
- 2 tablespoons fresh lime juice
- 1 tablespoon low-sodium soy sauce
- ½ tablespoon chili paste
- Salt, as required

For Sauce:

- 1½ cups homemade beef broth
- 1 tablespoon low-sodium soy sauce
- ½ tablespoon red boat fish sauce

Preparation:

1. For meatballs: in a large bowl, add all the ingredients and with your hands, mix until well combined.

2. Make golf ball-sized meatballs from the mixture and arrange onto a large parchment paper-lined baking sheet.

3. Freeze for about 20 minutes.

4. In the pot of Ninja Foodi, place the meatballs and top with broth, soy sauce and fish sauce.

5. Close the Ninja Foodi with the pressure lid and place the pressure valve to "Seal" position.

6. Select "Pressure" and set to "High for 5 minutes.

7. Press "Start/Stop" to begin cooking.

8. Switch the valve to "Vent" and do a "Natural" release.

9. Serve hot.

Nutrition Values Per Serving:

Calories: 192 Fats: 13.3g Net Carbs: 2g Carbs: 2.2g Fiber: 0.2g Sugar: 0.6g Proteins: 16.1g Sodium: 491mg

Cabbage & Pork Stew

Prepping Time: 15 minutes

Cooking time: 7½ hours

Servings: 8

Ingredients:

- 2½ pounds boneless country-style pork ribs
- 2½ cups cabbage, chopped
- 2 cups tomatoes, chopped finely
- 1 medium onion, chopped
- 2 garlic cloves, minced
- 2 tablespoon olive oil
- 4 cups homemade chicken broth
- 1 tablespoon fresh oregano, minced
- Salt and ground black pepper, as required
- 3 tablespoon fresh lime juice

Preparation:

In the pot of Ninja Foodi, add all ingredients and mix well. Close the Ninja Foodi with crisping lid and select "Slow Cooker". Set on "Low" for 7½ hours. Press "Start/Stop" to begin cooking. Transfer pork into large bowl and with 2 forks, shred the meat. Return the shredded pork into the pot and mix well.

Serve hot with the drizzling of lime juice.

Nutrition Values Per Serving:

Calories: 299 Fats: 15.8g Net Carbs: 3.8g Carbs: 5.4g Fiber: 1.6g Sugar: 2.8g Proteins: 31.2g Sodium: 496mg

Sausage & Pork Meatloaf

Prepping Time: 15 minutes

Cooking time: 25 minutes

Servings: 4

Ingredients:

- 14 ounces lean ground pork
- 1 gluten-free chorizo sausage, chopped finely
- 1 small onion, chopped
- 1 garlic clove, minced
- 2 tablespoons fresh cilantro, chopped
- 3 tablespoons pork rinds, crushed
- 1 organic egg
- Salt and ground black pepper, as required
- 2 tablespoons fresh mushrooms, sliced thinly

- 2 tablespoons olive oil

Preparation:

1. In a large bowl, add all ingredients except mushrooms and mix until well combined.
2. In a baking pan, place the beef mixture and with the back of a spatula, smooth the surface.
3. Top with mushroom slices and gently, press into the meatloaf.
4. Drizzle with oil evenly.
5. Arrange the "Reversible Rack" in the pot of Ninja Foodi.
6. Close the Ninja Foodi with crisping lid and select "Air Crisp".
7. Set the temperature to 390 degrees F for 5 minutes.
8. Press "Start/Stop" to begin preheating.
9. After preheating, open the lid.
10. Place the pan over the "Reversible Rack".
11. Close the Ninja Foodi with crisping lid and select "Air Crisp".
12. Set the temperature to 390 degrees F for 25 minutes.
13. Press "Start/Stop" to begin cooking.
14. Cut the meatloaf in desires size wedges and serve.

Nutrition Values Per Serving:

Calories: 320 Fats: 25.6g Net Carbs: 1.7g Carbs: 2.1g Fiber: 0.4g Sugar: 0.9g Proteins: 21.1g Sodium: 103mg

Lemony Pork Butt

Prepping Time: 45 minutes

Cooking time: 38 minutes

Servings: 5

Ingredients:

- 2 pounds pork butt, cut into 2-inch pieces
- Salt and ground black pepper, as required
- 2-3 tablespoons fresh lemon juice
- 1 yellow onion, peeled and cut in half
- ½ cup homemade chicken broth

Preparation:

Season the pork butt with salt and black pepper generously. In the pot of Ninja Foodi, place the pork butt. Place the lemon juice over pork butt. Place the onion and broth over the pork. Close the Ninja Foodi with pressure lid and place the pressure valve to "Seal" position. Select "Pressure" and set to "High" for 20 minutes. Press "Start/Stop" to begin cooking. Switch the valve to "Vent" and do a "Quick" release. Remove the onion from the pot. Select "Sauté/Sear" setting of Ninja Foodi and cook for about 10 minutes. Press "Start/Stop" to stop cooking. Now, close the Ninja Foodi with crisping lid and select "Broil" for 8 minutes. Press "Start/Stop" to begin cooking.

Serve hot.

Nutrition Values Per Serving:

Calories: 304 Fats: 10.3g Net Carbs: 1.5g Carbs: 1.9g Fiber: 0.4g Sugar: 1g Proteins: 47.7g Sodium: 177mg

Caramelized Pork Butt

Prepping Time: 45 minutes

Cooking time: 38 minutes

Servings: 6

Ingredients:

- 2 tablespoons olive oil
- 2 pounds pork butt, cut in 1-inch pieces
- Salt and ground black pepper, as required
- 4 tablespoons Erythritol
- 3 garlic cloves, minced
- 2 tablespoons red boat fish sauce
- ½ cup water
- ½ cup homemade chicken broth
- 1 small onion, sliced

Preparation:

1. Select "Sauté/Sear" setting of Ninja Foodi and place the butter into the pot. Press "Start/Stop" to begin cooking and heat for about 2-3 minutes. Add the pork, salt and black pepper and cook for about 4-5 minutes or until browned completely. Add the Erythritol and cook for about 2 minutes or until golden brown, stirring continuously. Stir in the garlic and cook for about 1 minute. Press "Start/Stop" to stop cooking and stir in the fish sauce, broth and water. Close the Ninja Foodi with the pressure lid and place the pressure valve to "Seal" position. Select "Pressure" and set to "High" for 20 minutes. Press "Start/Stop" to begin cooking. Switch the valve to "Vent" and do a "Natural" release. Select "Sauté/Sear" setting of Ninja Foodi and stir in the onions. Cook for about 5-10 minutes or until desired thickness of sauce.

2. Press "Start/Stop" to stop cooking and serve hot.

Nutrition Values Per Serving:

Calories: 347 Fats: 14.9g Net Carbs: 1.4g Carbs: 1.7g Fiber: 0.3g Sugar: 0.6g Proteins: 49g Sodium: 674mg

Cheesy Pork Sausage

Prepping Time: 15 minutes

Cooking time: 20 minutes

Servings: 6

Ingredients:

- 2 pounds gluten-free pork sausages, casing removed and crumbled
- 16 ounces sugar-free marinara sauce
- 10 ounces Parmesan cheese, shredded

- 16 ounces mozzarella cheese, shredded

Preparation:

1. Close the Ninja Foodi with crisping lid and select "Bake/Roast".
2. Set the temperature to 360 degrees F for 5 minutes.
3. Press "Start/Stop" to begin preheating.
4. After preheating, open the lid.
5. Grease the pot of Ninja Foodi generously.
6. In the prepared pot, arrange half of the sausages and top with half of the marinara sauce, followed by half of the mozzarella and Parmesan cheese.
7. Repeat the layer once.
8. Close the Ninja Foodi with crisping lid and select "Bake/Roast".
9. Set the temperature to 360 degrees F for 20 minutes.
10. Press "Start/Stop" to begin cooking.
11. Serve hot.

Nutrition Values Per Serving:

Calories: 916 Fats: 68g Net Carbs: 7g Carbs: 9g Fiber: 2g Sugar: 3.2g Proteins: 65g Sodium: 2000mg

Jamaican Pulled Pork

Prepping Time: 15 minutes

Cooking time: 55 minutes

Servings: 12

Ingredients:

- 4 pounds pork shoulder
- Olive oil cooking spray
- ¼ cup sugar-free Jamaican jerk spice blend
- 1 tablespoon butter
- ½ cup homemade beef broth

Preparation:

Spray the pork shoulder with the cooking spray and then, rub with Jamaican Jerk spice blend evenly. Select "Sauté/Sear" setting of Ninja Foodi and place the butter into the pot. Press "Start/Stop" to begin cooking and heat for about 2-3 minutes. Add the pork shoulder and cook, uncovered for about 10 minutes or until browned completely. Press "Start/Stop" to stop cooking and stir in the broth. Close the Ninja Foodi with pressure lid and place the pressure valve to "Seal" position. Select "Pressure" and set to "High" for 45 minutes. Press "Start/Stop" to begin cooking. Switch the valve to "Vent" and do a "Quick" release. With 2 forks, shred the meat and serve hot.

Nutrition Values Per Serving:

Calories: 479 Fats: 36.3g Net Carbs: 0.1g Carbs: 0.1g Fiber: 0g Sugar: 0.1g Proteins: 35.6g Sodium: 194mg

Delicious Pork & Bacon Chili

Prepping Time: 15 minutes

Cooking time: 6 hours 8 minutes

Servings: 8

Ingredients:

- 1 teaspoon olive oil
- 2 pounds ground pork
- 8 thick bacon slices, chopped
- 1 (14-ounce can diced tomatoes, drained
- 1 onion, chopped
- 3 small green bell peppers, chopped
- 1 (6-ounce can sugar-free tomato sauce
- 2 tablespoons red chili powder
- ¼ teaspoon garlic powder
- ¼ teaspoon onion powder
- Salt and ground black pepper, as required

Preparation:

1. Select "Sauté/Sear" setting of Ninja Foodi and place the oil into the pot.

2. Press "Start/Stop" to begin cooking and heat for about 2-3 minutes. Add the pork and cook for about 6-8 minutes or until browned completely.

3. Press "Start/Stop" to stop cooking and stir in the remaining ingredients.

4. Close the Ninja Foodi with crisping lid and select "Slow Cooker". Set on "Low" for 6 hours. Press "Start/Stop" to begin cooking.

5. Serve hot.

Nutrition Values Per Serving:

Calories: 290 Fats: 20.1g Net Carbs: 4.4g Carbs: 6.7g Fiber: 2.3g Sugar: 3.6g Proteins: 22.1g Sodium: 228mg

Tasty Ground Pork Soup

Prepping Time: 15 minutes

Cooking time: 30 minutes

Servings: 6

Ingredients:

- 1 tablespoon olive oil
- 1½ pounds ground pork
- 1 onion, chopped
- 2 cups carrots, peeled and chopped
- 2 cups green beans, trimmed and cut into pieces
- 5 cups homemade chicken broth

- 2/3 cup low-sodium soy sauce
- Ground black pepper, as required

Preparation:

Select "Sauté/Sear" setting of Ninja Foodi and place the butter into the pot. Press "Start/Stop" to begin cooking and heat for about 2-3 minutes. Add the pork and cook for about 5 minutes or until browned completely. Press "Start/Stop" to stop cooking and stir in the remaining ingredients. Close the Ninja Foodi with pressure lid and place the pressure valve to "Seal" position. Select "Pressure" and set to "High" for 25 minutes. Press "Start/Stop" to begin cooking. Switch the valve to "Vent" and do a "Quick" release.

Serve hot.

Nutrition Values Per Serving:

Calories: 303 Fats: 19.4g Net Carbs: 6.5g Carbs: 9g Fiber: 2.5g Sugar: 4.6g Proteins: 23.8g Sodium: 1600mg

Sweet & Sour Pork Butt

Prepping Time: 70 minutes

Cooking time: 1 hour

Servings: 6

Ingredients:

- 1 tablespoon garlic, minced
- ¼ cup red boat fish sauce
- 1 tablespoon fresh lime juice
- 2 tablespoons Erythritol
- 1 teaspoon five-spice powder
- Ground black pepper, as required
- 2½ pounds pork butt

Preparation:

For sauce: in a bowl, place the pork butt and top with the sauce evenly. Close the Ninja Foodi with the pressure lid and place the pressure valve to "Seal" position. Select "Pressure" and set to "High" for 60 minutes. Press "Start/Stop" to begin cooking. Switch the valve to "Vent" and do a "Natural" release. With tongs, place the pork butt onto a cutting board for about 5 minutes.

Cut into desired sized slices and serve with the topping of pan sauce.

Nutrition Values Per Serving:

Calories: 283 Fats: 9.5g Net Carbs: 0.4g Carbs: 0.4g Fiber: 0g Sugar: 0g Proteins: 46.2g Sodium: 873mg

Tasty Pork Stew

Prepping Time: 15 minutes

Cooking time: 50 minutes

Servings: 8

Ingredients:

- 1 tablespoon coconut oil
- ¼ pound shiitake mushrooms, stems removed and halved
- ¼ cup shallots, sliced thinly
- 4 garlic cloves, smashed
- 1 tablespoon fresh ginger, sliced
- 3 pounds pork shoulder, cubed into 2-inch size
- 3 tablespoons red boat fish sauce
- 1 cup homemade chicken broth
- 3 carrots, peeled and cut into ½-inch slices diagonally
- ½ cup fresh cilantro, chopped

Preparation:

Select "Sauté/Sear" setting of Ninja Foodi and place the butter into the pot. Press "Start/Stop" to begin cooking and heat for about 2-3 minutes. Add the mushrooms and shallots and cook for about 3-5 minutes. Stir in the garlic and ginger and cook for about 1 minute. Add the pork cubes and cook for about 1-2 minutes. Press "Start/Stop" to stop cooking and stir in the fish sauce and broth. Close the Ninja Foodi with the pressure lid and place the pressure valve to "Seal" position. Select "Pressure" and set to "High" for 40 minutes. Press "Start/Stop" to begin cooking. Switch the valve to "Vent" and do a "Natural" release. With a slotted spoon, transfer the pork cubes into a bowl. In the pot, add the carrots and stir to combine. Close the Ninja Foodi with the pressure lid and place the pressure valve to "Seal" position. Select "Pressure" and set to "High" for 10 minutes. Press "Start/Stop" to begin cooking. Switch the valve to "Vent" and do a "Quick" release. Stir in in the pork cubes and cilantro and serve hot.

Nutrition Values Per Serving:

Calories: 547 Fats: 38.4g Net Carbs: 5g Carbs: 6g Fiber: 1g Sugar: 1.8g Proteins: 42.2g Sodium: 821mg

Sausage & Green Beans

Prepping Time: 15 minutes

Cooking time: 25 minutes

Servings: 6

Ingredients:

- 4 cups fresh green beans, trimmed
- 1½ cups gluten-free cocktail sausages
- Salt and ground black pepper, as required
- 1 tablespoon olive oil

Preparation:

1. In a bowl, al all the ingredients and toss to coat well.
2. Arrange the foil-lined "Cook & Crisp Basket" in the pot of Ninja Foodi.
3. Close the Ninja Foodi with crisping lid and select "Air Crisp".
4. Set the temperature to 355 degrees F for 5 minutes.

5. Press "Start/Stop" to begin preheating.
6. After preheating, open the lid.
7. Place the sausage mixture into the "Cook & Crisp Basket".
8. Close the Ninja Foodi with crisping lid and select "Air Crisp".
9. Set the temperature to 355 degrees F for 25 minutes.
10. Press "Start/Stop" to begin cooking.
11. Flip the sausage mixture once halfway through.
12. Serve hot.

Nutrition Values Per Serving:

Calories: 235 Fats: 18.4g Net Carbs: 3g Carbs: 5.5g Fiber: 2.5g Sugar: 1g Proteins: 12.4g Sodium: 429mg

Sausage with Bell Peppers & Tomatoes

Prepping Time: 20 minutes

Cooking time: 6 hours

Servings: 6

Ingredients:

- 1¼ pounds gluten-free sausage, sliced
- 2 medium bell peppers, seeded and sliced
- 2 cups tomatoes, chopped finely
- 1 medium yellow onion, sliced
- Salt and ground black pepper, as required

Preparation:

1. In the pot of Ninja Foodi, place all the ingredients and stir to combine.
2. Close the Ninja Foodi with crisping lid and select "Slow Cooker".
3. Set on "Low" for 6 hours.
4. Press "Start/Stop" to begin cooking.
5. Serve hot.

Nutrition Values Per Serving:

Calories: 416 Fats: 32.4g Net Carbs: 4.9g Carbs: 7.1g Fiber: 2.2g Sugar: 4g Proteins: 23.3g Sodium: 855mg

Cheddar Meatballs

Prepping Time: 15 minutes

Cooking time: 14 minutes

Servings: 2

Ingredients:

- ½ pound ground pork
- 1 onion, chopped

- 1 teaspoon garlic paste
- 2 tablespoons fresh basil, chopped
- 1 teaspoon mustard
- 1 teaspoon yacon syrup
- 1 tablespoon Cheddar cheese, grated
- Salt and ground black pepper, as required

Preparation:

1. In a bowl, add all ingredients and mix until well combined.
2. Make small equal-sized balls from the mixture.
3. Arrange the greased "Cook & Crisp Basket" in the pot of Ninja Foodi
4. Close the Ninja Foodi with crisping lid and select "Air Crisp"
5. Set the temperature to 390 degrees F for 5 minutes.
6. Press "Start/Stop" to begin preheating.
7. After preheating, open the lid.
8. Place the meatballs into the "Cook & Crisp Basket".
9. Close the Ninja Foodi with crisping lid and select "Air Crisp".
10. Set the temperature to 390 degrees F for 14 minutes.
11. Press "Start/Stop" to begin cooking.
12. Serve hot.

Nutrition Values Per Serving:

Calories: 205 Fats: 5.7g Net Carbs: 4.3g Carbs: 5.4g Fiber: 1.1g Sugar: 2.2g Proteins: 31.5g Sodium: 89mg

Pork & Carrot Chili

Prepping Time: 15 minutes

Cooking time: 5 hours 5 minutes

Servings: 6

Ingredients:

- 1 teaspoon olive oil
- 1½ pounds ground pork
- 1 green bell pepper, seeded and chopped
- 1 small onion, chopped
- 2 large carrots, peeled and chopped
- 26 ounces fresh tomatoes, chopped finely
- 4 teaspoons chili powder
- 1 teaspoon paprika
- 1 teaspoon ground cumin
- 1 teaspoon garlic powder
- 1 teaspoon onion powder
- 1 tablespoon fresh parsley, chopped

- Salt and ground black pepper, as required
- 1 tablespoon Worcestershire sauce

Preparation:

Select "Sauté/Sear" setting of Ninja Foodi and place the butter into the pot. Press "Start/Stop" to begin cooking and heat for about 2-3 minutes. Add the pork and cook for about 5 minutes or until browned completely. Press "Start/Stop" to stop cooking and stir in the remaining ingredients. Close the Ninja Foodi with crisping lid and select "Slow Cooker". Set on "High" for 5 hours. Press "Start/Stop" to begin cooking.

Serve hot.

Nutrition Values Per Serving:

Calories: 211 Fats: 28.4.6g Net Carbs: 6.8g Carbs: 10g Fiber: 3.2g Sugar: 5g Proteins: 31.5g Sodium: 289mg

Bell Peppers & Cajun Sausage

Prepping Time: 15 minutes

Cooking time: 20 minutes

Servings: 6

Ingredients:

- 1½ pounds gluten-free sausages, cut into ½-inch size rounds
- 3 bell peppers, seeded and sliced
- ¼ cup onion, chopped
- ½ tablespoon Cajun seasoning

Preparation:

1. In a bowl, al all the ingredients and toss to coat well.
2. Arrange the foil-lined "Cook & Crisp Basket" in the pot of Ninja Foodi.
3. Close the Ninja Foodi with crisping lid and select "Air Crisp".
4. Set the temperature to 390 degrees F for 5 minutes.
5. Press "Start/Stop" to begin preheating.
6. After preheating, open the lid.
7. Place the sausage mixture into the "Cook & Crisp Basket".
8. Close the Ninja Foodi with crisping lid and select "Air Crisp".
9. Set the temperature to 390 degrees F for 20 minutes.
10. Press "Start/Stop" to begin cooking.
11. Flip the sausage mixture once halfway through.
12. Serve hot.

Nutrition Values Per Serving:

Calories: 398 Fats: 32.3g Net Carbs: 2.1g Carbs: 3.2g Fiber: 1.1g Sugar: 1.6g Proteins: 22.6g Sodium: 884mg

Pork and Eggplant Casserole

Prepping Time: 20 minutes

Cooking time: 3 hours

Servings: 10

Ingredients:

- 2 cups eggplant cubed
- Salt, as required
- 1 tablespoon olive oil
- 2 pounds lean ground pork
- 2 teaspoons Worcestershire sauce
- 2 teaspoons mustard
- Ground black pepper, as required
- 28 ounces canned diced tomatoes drained
- 16 ounces canned tomato sauce
- 2 cups mozzarella cheese, grated
- 2 tablespoons fresh parsley, chopped
- 1 teaspoon dried oregano

Preparation:

1. Select "Sauté/Sear" setting of Ninja Foodi and place the butter into the pot.
2. Press "Start/Stop" to begin cooking and heat for about 2-3 minutes.
3. Add the pork and cook for about 5 minutes or until browned completely.
4. In a colander, place the eggplant and sprinkle with salt.
5. Set aside for about 30 minutes.
6. Transfer the eggplant into bowl and mix with olive oil.
7. In another bowl, add the pork, Worcestershire sauce, mustard, salt and black pepper and mix well.
8. In the greased pot of Ninja Foodi, place the pork mixture and top with eggplant.
9. Spread tomatoes and sauce over eggplant and sprinkle with cheese, followed by parsley and oregano.
10. Close the Ninja Foodi with crisping lid and select "Slow Cooker".
11. Set on "High" for 3 hours.
12. Press "Start/Stop" to begin cooking.
13. Serve hot.

Nutrition Values Per Serving:

Calories: 192 Fats: 6.1g Net Carbs: g Carbs: 7.3g Fiber: 2.44.9g Sugar: 3.6g Proteins: 22.1g Sodium: 355mg

Chapter 4-Chicken and Poultry Recipes

Chicken and Cauliflower Rice Soup

Prepping time: 10 minutes

Cooking time: 31 minutes

Servings: 8

Ingredients:

- 1 cup cauliflower rice
- 1 pound chicken drumsticks
- 1 tablespoon salt
- 1 teaspoon curry
- 1 teaspoon dill
- 1 teaspoon ground celery root
- 1 garlic clove
- 3 tablespoons sour cream
- 1 teaspoon cilantro
- 6 cups of water
- ½ cup tomato juice
- 1 teaspoon oregano
- 1 tablespoon butter
- 8 ounces kale

Preparation:

Combine the salt, curry, dill, ground celery, and cilantro together in a mixing bowl and stir. Peel the garlic clove and slice it. Set the pressure cooker to «Pressure" mode. Add the butter into the pressure cooker and melt it. Add the sliced garlic and cook the dish for 30 seconds. Add the spice mixture and cook the dish for 10 seconds, stirring constantly. Add the drumsticks, sour cream, water, oregano, tomato juice, and cauliflower rice. Chop the kale and sprinkle the soup with it, stir well, and close the lid. Cook the dish on "Sauté" mode for 30 minutes. When the cooking time ends, open the pressure cooker lid, chill the soup briefly, then ladle it into serving bowls.

Nutrition Values Per Serving:

calories 140, fat 5.7, fiber 1, carbs 4.9, protein 17.1

Bacon-Wrapped Chicken Breasts

Prepping time: 20 mins

Cooking Time: 20 mins

Servings: 4

Ingredients:

- 1 tablespoon sugar
- 8 fresh basil leaves

- 2 tablespoons red boat fish sauce
- 2 tablespoons water
- 2 (8-ounce) boneless chicken breasts, cut each breast in half horizontally
- Salt and ground black pepper, as required
- 8 bacon strips
- 1 tablespoon honey

Preparation:

1. In a small heavy-bottomed pan, add the sugar over medium-low heat and cook for about 2-3 minutes or caramelized, stirring continuously.

2. Stir in the basil, fish sauce, and water.

3. Remove from heat and transfer into a large bowl.

4. Sprinkle the chicken with salt and black pepper.

5. Add the chicken pieces in the basil mixture and coat generously.

6. Refrigerate to marinate for about 4-6 hours.

7. Wrap each chicken piece with 2 bacon strips.

8. Coat each chicken piece with honey slightly.

9. Arrange the greased "Cook & Crisp Basket" in the pot of Ninja Foodi.

10. Close the Ninja Foodi with a crisping lid and select "Air Crisp."

11. Set the temperature to 365 degrees F for 5 minutes.

12. Press "Start/Stop" to begin preheating.

13. After preheating, open the lid.

14. Place the chicken breasts into the "Cook & Crisp Basket."

15. Close the Ninja Foodi with a crisping lid and select "Air Crisp."

16. Set the temperature to 365 degrees F for 20 minutes.

17. Press "Start/Stop" to begin cooking.

18. Open the lid and serve hot.

Nutrition Values Per Serving:

Calories: 564, Fat: 32.6 g, Saturated Fat: 10.3 g, Trans Fat: 22.3 g, Carbohydrates: 8.2 g, Fiber 0 g, Sodium 2100 mg, Protein: 56.3 g

Tasty Chicken Tart

Prepping time: 10 minutes

Cooking time: 35 minutes

Servings: 8

Ingredients:

- 1 cup almond flour
- 1 egg
- 7 ounces butter
- 1 teaspoon salt
- 10 ounces ground chicken

- 1 teaspoon olive oil
- 1 red onion
- 1 tablespoon cream
- 1 teaspoon ground pepper
- 4 ounces celery stalk

Preparation:

Combine the almond flour and butter together in a mixing bowl. Add the egg and knead the dough. Put the dough in the freezer. Peel the onion and grate it. Combine the onion with the salt, ground chicken, cream, ground pepper. Chop the celery stalk and add it to the ground chicken mixture and stir. Set the pressure cooker to "Pressure" mode. Spray the pressure cooker with the olive oil. Remove the dough from the freezer and cut it in half. Grate the first part of the dough into the pressure cooker. Add half of the chicken mixture. Grate the remaining dough and add the remaining chicken mixture. Close the pressure cooker lid and cook for 35 minutes. When the dish is cooked, let it rest briefly. Slice the tart and serve.

Nutrition Values Per Serving:

calories 348, fat 31, fiber 2.1, carbs 5, protein 14.4

Spinach Stuffed Chicken Breasts

Prepping time: 15 mins

Cooking Time: 30 mins

Servings: 2

Ingredients:
- 1 tablespoon olive oil
- 1¾ ounces fresh spinach
- ¼ cup ricotta cheese, shredded
- 2 (4-ounce) skinless, boneless chicken breasts
- Salt and ground black pepper, as required
- 2 tablespoons cheddar cheese, grated
- ¼ teaspoon paprika

Preparation:
1. Select the "Sauté/Sear" setting of Ninja Foodi and place the oil into the pot.
2. Press "Start/Stop" to begin cooking and heat for about 2-3 minutes.
3. Add the spinach and cook for about 3-4 minutes.
4. Stir in the ricotta and cook for about 40-60 seconds.
5. Press "Start/Stop" to stop cooking and transfer the spinach mixture into a bowl.
6. Set aside to cool.
7. Cut slits into the chicken breasts about ¼-inch apart but not all the way through.
8. Stuff each chicken breast with the spinach mixture.
9. Sprinkle each chicken breast with salt and black pepper and then with cheddar cheese and paprika.

10. Arrange the greased "Cook & Crisp Basket" in the pot of Ninja Foodi.

11. Close the Ninja Foodi with a crisping lid and select "Air Crisp."

12. Set the temperature to 390 degrees F for 5 minutes.

13. Press "Start/Stop" to begin preheating.

14. After preheating, open the lid.

15. Place the chicken breasts into the "Cook & Crisp Basket."

16. Close the Ninja Foodi with a crisping lid and select "Air Crisp."

17. Set the temperature to 390 degrees F for 25 minutes.

18. Press "Start/Stop" to begin cooking.

19. Open the lid and serve hot.

Nutrition Values Per Serving:

Calories: 279, Fat: 16 g, Saturated Fat: 5.6 g, Trans Fat: 10.4 g, Carbohydrates: 2.7 g, Fiber 0.7 g, Sodium 220 mg, Protein: 31.4 g

Lemony Whole Chicken

Prepping time: 15 mins

Cooking Time: 1 hour 29 minutes

Servings: 10

Ingredients:

• 1 (6-pound) whole chicken, necks and giblets removed

• Salt and ground black pepper, as required

• 3 fresh rosemary sprigs, divided

• 1 lemon, zested and cut into quarters

• 2 large onions, sliced,

• 4 cups chicken broth

Preparation:

1. Stuff the cavity of chicken with 2 rosemary sprigs and lemon quarters.

2. Season the chicken with salt and black pepper evenly.

3. Chop the remaining rosemary sprig and set aside.

4. Select "Sauté/Sear" setting of Ninja Foodi and place the chicken into the pot.

5. Press "Start/Stop" to begin and cook, uncovered for about 5-7 minutes per side.

6. Remove chicken from the pot and place onto a roasting rack.

7. In the pot, place the onions and broth.

8. Arrange the "Reversible Rack" over the broth mixture.

9. Arrange the roasting rack on top of "Reversible Rack".

10. Sprinkle the chicken with reserved chopped rosemary and lemon zest.

11. Close the Ninja Foodi with crisping lid and select "Bake/Roast".

12. Set the temperature to 375 degrees F for 1¼ hours.

13. Press "Start/Stop" to begin cooking.

14. Open the lid and place the chicken onto a cutting board for about 10 minutes before carving.

15. Cut into desired sized pieces and serve.

Nutrition Values Per Serving:

Calories: 545, Fat: 20.8 g, Saturated Fat: 5.7 g, Trans Fat: 15.1 g, Carbohydrates: 3.3 g, Sodium 556 mg, Protein: 81 g

Glazed Chicken Drumsticks

Prepping time: 15 mins

Cooking Time: 25 mins

Servings: 4

Ingredients:

- ¼ cup Dijon mustard
- 1 tablespoon honey
- 2 tablespoons olive oil
- Salt and ground black pepper, as required
- 4 (6 ounces) chicken drumsticks

Preparation:

1. In a bowl, add all the ingredients except the drumsticks and mix until well combined.
2. Add the drumsticks and coat with the mixture generously.
3. Refrigerate, covered to marinate overnight.
4. In the pot of Ninja Foodi, place 1 cup of water.
5. Arrange the greased "Cook & Crisp Basket" in the pot of Ninja Foodi.
6. Place the chicken drumsticks into the "Cook & Crisp Basket."
7. Close the Ninja Foodi with the pressure lid and place the pressure valve to the "Seal" position.
8. Select "Pressure" and set it to "High" for 6 minutes.
9. Press "Start/Stop" to begin cooking.
10. Switch the valve to "Vent" and do a "Quick" release.
11. Now, close the Ninja Foodi with a crisping lid and Select "Air Crisp."
12. Set the temperature to 320 degrees F for 12 minutes.
13. Press "Start/Stop" to begin cooking.
14. After 12 minutes of cooking, set the temperature to 355 degrees F for 5 minutes.
15. Open the lid and serve hot.

Nutrition Values Per Serving:

Calories: 374, Fat: 17.3 g, Saturated Fat: 3.6 g, Trans Fat: 13.6 g, Carbohydrates: 5.2 g, Fiber 0.5 g, Sodium 352 mg, Protein: 47.5 g

Crispy Duck Patties

Prepping time: 10 minutes

Cooking time: 15 minutes

Servings: 6

Ingredients:

- 1 tablespoon mustard
- 1 teaspoon ground black pepper
- 9 ounces ground duck
- ½ cup parsley
- 1 teaspoon salt
- 1 tablespoon olive oil
- 1 teaspoon oregano
- 1 teaspoon red pepper
- ½ teaspoon cayenne pepper
- 1 tablespoon flax meal

Preparation:

Combine the mustard, ground black pepper, ground duck, salt, oregano, red pepper, cayenne pepper, and flax meal together in a mixing bowl and stir well. Wash the parsley and chop it. Sprinkle the duck mixture with the chopped parsley and stir well. Make medium-sized patties from the duck mixture. Set the pressure cooker to "Sauté" mode. Pour the olive oil into the pressure cooker. Add the duck patties and cook the dish on sauté mode for 15 minutes or until browned on both sides. Serve immediately.

Nutrition Values Per Serving:

calories 106, fat 6.9, fiber 1.3 carbs 3.3, protein 8.6

Turkey with Chickpeas & Quinoa

Prepping time: 15 mins

Cooking Time: 20 mins

Servings: 4

Ingredients:

- 1½ tablespoons olive oil
- 6 ounces skinless, boneless turkey breast, cubed
- 1 medium onion, chopped
- 1 small sweet potato, peeled and chopped
- 2 garlic cloves, minced
- 1 tablespoon red chili powder
- ¼ teaspoon red pepper flakes, crushed
- ¼ teaspoon ground cumin
- ¼ teaspoon ground coriander
- Salt, to taste
- 1 cup canned chickpeas, rinsed and drained
- ¼ cup uncooked quinoa
- 1 cup tomatoes, chopped finely
- 1½ cups chicken broth

- 1 tablespoon fresh lemon juice
- 2 tablespoons fresh cilantro, chopped

Preparation:

1. Select "Sauté/Sear" setting of Ninja Foodi and place the oil into the pot.
2. Press "Start/Stop" to begin cooking and heat for about 2-3 minutes.
3. Add the turkey and cook for about 5 minutes or until browned completely.
4. With a slotted spoon, transfer the turkey into a bowl.
5. In the pot, add the onion and cook for about 5 minutes.
6. Add the sweet potato and cook for about 5 minutes.
7. Add the garlic and spices and cook for about 1 minute.
8. Press "Start/Stop" to stop cooking and stir in the turkey, chickpeas, quinoa, tomato and broth.
9. Close the Ninja Foodi with the pressure lid and place the pressure valve to "Seal" position.
10. Select "Pressure" and set to "High for 4 minutes.
11. Press "Start/Stop" to begin cooking.
12. Do a "Natural" release for about 10 minutes and then switch the valve to "Vent" to do a "Quick" release.
13. Open the lid and stir in the lemon juice and cilantro.
14. Serve hot.

Nutrition Values Per Serving:

Calories: 390, Fat: 11.5 g, Saturated Fat: 1.9 g, Trans Fat: 9.6 g, Carbohydrates: 49.8 g, Fiber 12.3 g, Sodium 387 mg, Protein: 24.2 g

Warm Chicken Salad

Prepping time: 10 minutes

Cooking time: 25 minutes

Servings: 7

Ingredients:

- 1 pound boneless chicken
- 1 cup spinach
- 1 tablespoon mayonnaise
- 1 teaspoon lemon juice
- 4 eggs, boiled
- 1 tablespoon chives
- ½ cup dill

Preparation:

Put the chicken in the trivet and place the trivet into the pressure cooker. Set the pressure cooker to "Steam" mode. Cook the dish for 25 minutes. Peel the eggs and chop them. Chop the spinach and dill. Transfer the chopped greens to a mixing bowl. Add chives and chopped eggs. Sprinkle the mixture with the lemon juice and mayonnaise. When the chicken is cooked, remove it from the pressure cooker and let it rest briefly. Grind the cooked chicken and transfer it to the egg mixture. Mix until smooth and serve.

Nutrition Values Per Serving:

calories 154, fat 8, fiber 0, carbs 0.92, protein 19

Asian-style Chicken Strips

Prepping time: 10 minutes

Cooking time: 30 minutes

Servings: 7

Ingredients:

- ½ cup of soy sauce
- 1 tablespoon liquid stevia
- 1 tablespoon sesame seeds
- ½ cup chicken stock
- 1 tablespoon oregano
- 1 teaspoon cumin
- 1 pound boneless chicken breast
- 1 teaspoon butter

Preparation:

Cut the chicken breast into the strips and transfer the strips to the mixing bowl. Combine the soy sauce and liquid stevia in a mixing bowl. Stir the mixture. Add sesame seeds, chicken stock, oregano, cumin, and butter. Whisk the mixture and combine it with the chicken strips. Let the chicken strips marinate for 10 minutes. Set the pressure cooker to "Pressure" mode. Transfer the chicken strips mixture to the pressure cooker. Close the lid and cook for 30 minutes. When the dish is cooked, release the pressure and open the pressure cooker lid. Transfer the chicken strips and soy sauce mixture to serving bowls.

Nutrition Values Per Serving:

calories 149, fat 6.2, fiber 0.6, carbs 2.3, protein 20.3

Garlic Chicken Thighs

Prepping time: 15 minutes

Cooking time: 40 minutes

Servings: 6

Ingredients:

- 1 tablespoon garlic powder
- ⅓ cup garlic
- ½ lemon
- 1 teaspoon onion powder
- 2 tablespoons mayonnaise
- 1 teaspoon ground white pepper

- 1 tablespoon butter
- 1 teaspoon cayenne pepper
- pound 1 pound chicken thighs
- 4 ounces celery root

Preparation:

Peel the garlic cloves and mince them. Combine the garlic with the chicken thighs and using a combine using your hands. Sprinkle the meat with the onion powder, ground white pepper, cayenne pepper, and butter. Peel the celery root and grate it. Chop the lemon into thin slices. Add the celery root and lemon in the chicken mixture. Add garlic powder and mayonnaise, stir well and transfer it to the pressure cooker. Set the pressure cooker to "Sear/Sauté" mode. Close the lid and cook the dish on poultry mode for 40 minutes. When the cooking time ends, open the pressure cooker lid and transfer the cooked chicken into serving bowls.

Nutrition Values Per Serving:

calories 142, fat 5.7, fiber 1, carbs 5.7, protein 17

Amazing Parsley Duck Legs

Prepping time: 10 mins

Cooking Time: 30 mins

Servings: 2

Ingredients:

- 2 garlic cloves, minced
- 1 tablespoon fresh parsley, chopped
- 1 teaspoon five-spice powder
- Salt and ground black pepper, as required
- 2 duck legs

Preparation:

1. In a bowl, mix together garlic, parsley, five-spice powder, salt and black pepper.
2. Rub the duck legs with garlic mixture generously.
3. Arrange the "Cook & Crisp Basket" in the pot of Ninja Foodi.
4. Close the Ninja Foodi with crisping lid and select "Air Crisp".
5. Set the temperature to 340 degrees F for 5 minutes.
6. Press "Start/Stop" to begin preheating.
7. After preheating, open the lid.
8. Place the duck legs into the "Cook & Crisp Basket".
9. Close the Ninja Foodi with crisping lid and select "Air Crisp".
10. Set the temperature to 340 degrees F for 25 minutes.
11. Press "Start/Stop" to begin cooking.
12. After 25 minutes of cooking, set the temperature to 390 degrees F for 5 minutes.
13. Open the lid and serve hot.

Nutrition Values Per Serving:

Calories: 434, Fat: 14.4 g, Saturated Fat: 3.2 g, Trans Fat: 11.2 g, Carbohydrates: 1.1 g, Fiber: 0.1 g, Sodium: 339 mg, Protein: 70.4 g

Amazing Duck Pot Pie

Prepping time: 10 minutes

Cooking time: 50 minutes

Servings: 8

Ingredients:

- 7 ounces keto dough
- 1 teaspoon onion powder
- 1 pound duck breast
- ½ teaspoon anise
- 1 cup green beans
- 1 cup cream
- 1 egg
- 1 teaspoon salt

Preparation:

Place the duck breast on the trivet and transfer the trivet into the pressure cooker. Set the pressure cooker to "Steam" mode. Steam the duck for 25 minutes. When the cooking time ends, remove the duck from the pressure cooker and shred it well. Place the shredded duck in the mixing bowl. Add onion powder, anise, cream, salt, and green beans and stir well. Beat the egg. Roll the keto dough and cut it into two parts. Put the one part of the bread dough into the pressure cooker and make the pie crust. Transfer filling in the pie crust and cover it with the second part of the dough. Spread the pie with the whisked egg and close the lid. Cook the dish on "Pressure" mode for 25 minutes. When the cooking time ends, let the pot pie rest briefly. Transfer it to a serving plate, cut it into slices and serve.

Nutrition Values Per Serving:

calories 194, fat 5.6, fiber 3.8, carbs 7.8, protein 28

Heathy Chicken Meatballs

Prepping time: 10 minutes

Cooking time: 10 minutes

Servings: 8

Ingredients:

- 1 cup broccoli rice, cooked
- 10 ounces ground chicken
- 1 carrot
- 1 egg
- 1 teaspoon salt
- ½ teaspoon cayenne pepper

- 1 teaspoon olive oil
- 1 tablespoon flax meal
- 1 teaspoon sesame oil

Preparation:

Peel the carrot and chop it roughly. Transfer the chopped carrot to a blender and blend it well. Combine the blended carrot and ground chicken together in a mixing bowl and stir. Sprinkle the meat mixture with the broccoli rice, egg, cayenne pepper, salt, and flax meal and combine well. Set the pressure cooker to "Sauté" mode. Pour the olive oil and sesame oil into the pressure cooker. Make meatballs from the meat mixture and place them into the pressure cooker. Cook the dish on sauté mode for 10 minutes. Stir the meatballs until all the sides are light brown. Remove them from the pressure cooker, drain on paper towel to remove any excess oil, and serve.

Nutrition Values Per Serving:

calories 96, fat 4.7, fiber 0.8, carbs 1.9, protein 11.5

Tomato Ground Chicken Bowl

Prepping time: 10 minutes

Cooking time: 30 minutes

Servings: 5

Ingredients:

- 1 cup tomatoes
- ½ cup cream
- 1 onion
- 1 teaspoon chili powder
- 3 tablespoons tomato paste
- 1 bell pepper
- 1 jalapeño pepper
- 1 tablespoon olive oil
- 15 ounces ground chicken

Preparation:

Peel the onion and dice it. Combine the onion with the chili powder, tomato paste, and cream and stir well. Chop the jalapeño pepper and bell pepper. Wash the tomatoes and chop them. Set the pressure cooker to "Sauté" mode. Place all the ingredients into the pressure cooker. Add ground chicken and combine. Close the pressure cooker lid and cook for 30 minutes. When the cooking time ends, remove the dish from the pressure cooker and stir well. Transfer the dish to serving bowls.

Nutrition Values Per Serving:

calories 220, fat 14.5, fiber 2, carbs 7.24, protein 17

Tasty Chicken Pies

Prepping time: 15 minutes

Cooking time: 24 minutes

Servings: 8

Ingredients:

- 8 ounces puff pastry
- 4 ounces ground chicken
- 1 teaspoon paprika
- 1 teaspoon ground ginger
- ½ teaspoon cilantro
- 1 egg
- 1 tablespoon butter
- 1 onion
- 1 teaspoon olive oil

Preparation:

Roll the puff pastry using a rolling pin. Cut the rolled puff pastry into medium-sized squares. Combine the ground chicken, cilantro, ground ginger, paprika, and egg together in a mixing bowl and stir well. Peel the onion and dice it. Add the onion to the meat mixture and stir well. Place the ground chicken mixture in the middle of every square and wrap them to form the pies. Set the pressure cooker to "Sear/Sauté" mode. Spray the pressure cooker with the olive oil inside and place the chicken pies inside. Close the pressure cooker lid and cook the dish for 24 minutes. When the chicken pies are cooked, remove them from the pressure cooker, let it rest briefly and serve.

Nutrition Values Per Serving:

calories 217, fat 15.2, fiber 1, carbs 14.52, protein 6

Chicken Curry

Prepping time: 10 minutes

Cooking time: 21 minutes

Servings: 7

Ingredients:

- 1 teaspoon garam masala
- 1 tablespoon curry paste
- 1 teaspoon coriander
- 1 teaspoon ground cumin
- 1 onion
- 3 garlic cloves
- 1 pound chicken thighs
- 1 teaspoon ginger
- 1 tablespoon butter

- 1 cup tomatoes
- 1 teaspoon salt
- 3 cups chicken stock
- 3 tablespoons chives
- ¼ cup of coconut milk

Preparation:

Combine the garam masala, curry paste, and coriander in a mixing bowl. Stir the mixture and add the ground cumin, ginger, and salt and stir well. Set the pressure cooker to «Pressure" mode. Add the butter into the pressure cooker and add the spice mixture. Cook the mixture for 1 minute, stirring frequently. Peel the garlic and onion. Chop the vegetables and add them into the pressure cooker. Chop the tomatoes and add them into the pressure cooker. Sprinkle the mixture with the chives and mix well. Add the chicken thighs, coconut milk, and chicken stock. Close the pressure cooker lid and cook the dish on "Pressure" mode for 20 minutes. When the dish is cooked, remove the food from the pressure cooker, shred the chicken, and serve.

Nutrition Values Per Serving:

calories 160, fat 6.9, fiber 1, carbs 7.57, protein 17

Herbed Cornish Hen

Prepping time: 15 mins

Cooking Time: 16 mins

Servings: 6

Ingredients:

- ½ cup olive oil
- 1 teaspoon fresh rosemary, chopped
- 1 teaspoon fresh thyme, chopped
- 1 teaspoon fresh lemon zest, grated finely
- ¼ teaspoon sugar
- ¼ teaspoon red pepper flakes, crushed
- Salt and ground black pepper, as required
- 2 pounds Cornish game hen, backbone removed and halved

Preparation:

1. In a large bowl, mix well all ingredients except hen portions.
2. Add the hen portions and coat with marinade generously.
3. Cover and refrigerator for about 2-24 hours.
4. In a strainer, place the hen portions to drain any liquid.
5. Arrange the greased "Cook & Crisp Basket" in the pot of Ninja Foodi.
6. Close the Ninja Foodi with crisping lid and select "Air Crisp".
7. Set the temperature to 390 degrees F for 5 minutes.
8. Press "Start/Stop" to begin preheating.
9. After preheating, open the lid.

10. Place the hen portions into the "Cook & Crisp Basket".
11. Close the Ninja Foodi with crisping lid and select "Air Crisp".
12. Set the temperature to 390 degrees F for 16 minutes.
13. Press "Start/Stop" to begin cooking.
14. Open the lid and place the hen portions onto a cutting board.
15. Cut each portion in 2 pieces and serve hot.

Nutrition Values Per Serving:

Calories: 681, Fat: 57.4 g, Saturated Fat: 12.7 g, Trans Fat: 44.7 g, Carbohydrates: 0.8 g, Fiber 0.3 g, Sodium 180 mg, Protein: 38.2 g

Braised Turkey Breast

Prepping time: 15 mins

Cooking Time: 30 mins

Servings: 8

Ingredients:

- 1 celery stalk, chopped
- 1 large onion, chopped
- 1 tablespoon fresh thyme, minced
- 1 tablespoon fresh rosemary, minced
- 14 ounces chicken broth
- 1 (6½-pound) skin-on, bone-in turkey breast
- Salt and ground black pepper, as required
- 3 tablespoons cornstarch
- 3 tablespoons water

Preparation:

1. In the pot of Ninja Foodi, place celery, onion, herbs, and broth.
2. Arrange turkey breast on top and sprinkle with salt and black pepper.
3. Close the Ninja Foodi with the pressure lid and place the pressure valve to "Seal" position.
4. Select "Pressure" and set to "High" for 30 minutes.
5. Press "Start/Stop" to begin cooking.
6. Switch the valve to "Vent" and do a "Quick" release.
7. Open the lid and transfer the turkey breast onto a cutting board.
8. With a slotted spoon, skim off the fat from the surface of broth. Then strain it, discarding solids.
9. In a small bowl, dissolve the cornstarch in water.
10. Return the broth in pot and select "Sauté/Sear" setting of Ninja Foodi.
11. Press "Start/Stop" to begin cooking.
12. Add the cornstarch mixture, stirring continuously and cook for about 3-4 minutes.
13. Press "Start/Stop" to stop cooking and transfer the gravy into a serving bowl.
14. Cut the turkey breast into desired sized slices and serve alongside the gravy.

Nutrition Values Per Serving:

Calories: 655, Fat: 26.7 g, Saturated Fat: 6.7 g, Trans Fat: g, Carbohydrates: 5.2 g, Fiber 0.8 g, Sodium 641 mg, Protein: 80.3 g

Stuffed Tomatoes with Ground Chicken

Prepping time: 10 minutes

Cooking time: 10 minutes

Servings: 6

Ingredients:

- 5 big tomatoes
- 10 ounces ground chicken
- 1 teaspoon ground black pepper
- 1 tablespoon sour cream
- 6 ounces Parmesan cheese
- 1 onion
- 1 tablespoon minced garlic
- 5 tablespoon chicken stock
- 1 teaspoon cayenne pepper

Preparation:

Use a paring knife or apple corer to remove the flesh from the tomatoes. Combine the ground chicken, ground black pepper, sour cream, minced garlic, and cayenne pepper together in a mixing bowl. Peel the onion and grate it. Add the onion to the ground chicken mixture and stir well. Fill the tomatoes with the ground chicken mixture. Grate the Parmesan cheese and sprinkle the stuffed tomatoes with the cheese. Set the pressure cooker to "Pressure" mode. Pour the chicken stock into the pressure cooker and add the stuffed tomatoes. Close the pressure cooker lid and cook for 20 minutes. When the cooking time ends, let the dish rest briefly. Transfer the tomatoes to a serving plate and serve.

Nutrition Values Per Serving:

calories 222, fat 12.4, fiber 1, carbs 10.55, protein 18

Butter Chicken Cutlets

Prepping time: 15 minutes

Cooking time: 25 minutes

Servings: 8

Ingredients:

- 3 tablespoons cream
- 5 tablespoon butter
- 1 teaspoon starch
- 2 tablespoons chicken stock
- 9 ounces ground chicken
- ½ cup dill

- 1 teaspoon ground black pepper
- 1 teaspoon paprika
- 1 teaspoon tomato paste
- 2 eggs
- 3 tablespoons semolina

Preparation:

Combine the cream and butter together and whisk. Sprinkle the mixture with the starch, paprika, tomato paste, semolina, and ground black pepper and stir well. Set the pressure cooker to "Sear/Sauté" mode. Chop the dill and add it into the pressure cooker. Add the eggs and ground chicken and combine. Make medium-sized balls from the ground chicken mixture, then flatten them. Pour the chicken stock into the pressure cooker and add the chicken flatten balls. Close the pressure cooker lid and cook for 25 minutes. When the dish is cooked, let it rest briefly and serve.

Nutrition Values Per Serving:

calories 172, fat 13.4, fiber 0, carbs 4.32, protein 9

Raspberries Chicken Fillets

Prepping time: 10 minutes

Cooking time: 25 minutes

Servings: 8

Ingredients:

- 8 ounces raspberries
- 1 pound boneless chicken breast
- 1 teaspoon sour cream
- ⅓ cup cream
- 6 ounces Parmesan
- 2 tablespoons butter
- 1 teaspoon cilantro
- 1 tablespoon white pepper

Preparation:

Pound the chicken breasts with a meat mallet. Set the pressure cooker to "Sauté" mode. Add the butter into the pressure cooker and melt it. Grate the Parmesan cheese. Sprinkle the chicken with the cilantro and white pepper. Place the boneless chicken breasts into the pressure cooker. Sprinkle them with raspberries. Add sour cream and cream. Sprinkle the dish with the grated cheese. Close the pressure cooker lid and cook the dish on "Sear/Sauté" mode for 25 minutes. When the cooking time ends, remove the dish from the pressure cooker, and let it rest, and serve.

Nutrition Values Per Serving:

calories 226, fat 12.5, fiber 2.1, carbs 5, protein 23.8

Chicken Piccata

Prepping time: 10 minutes

Cooking time: 17 minutes

Servings: 8

Ingredients:

- 2 tablespoons capers
- 1 ½ pound boneless chicken breast
- 1 teaspoon ground black pepper
- 3 tablespoons olive oil
- 3 tablespoons butter
- 1 teaspoon salt
- ½ cup lemon juice
- 1 cup chicken stock
- ⅓ cup fresh parsley
- 1 teaspoon oregano
- 1 tablespoon coconut flour
- 1 teaspoon paprika

Preparation:

Cut the chicken breast into medium-sized pieces. Sprinkle the chicken with the ground black pepper, salt, oregano, and paprika and stir well. Set the pressure cooker to "Sauté" mode. Pour the olive oil and butter into the pressure cooker. Stir well and sauté it for 1 minute. Add the chicken into the pressure cooker, and cook the chicken for 6 minutes. Stir the chicken frequently. Remove the chicken from the pressure cooker. Add the capers, lemon juice, chicken stock, and coconut flour to the pressure cooker and stir well until smooth. Cook the liquid for 1 minute. Add the cooked chicken and close the pressure cooker lid. Cook for 10 minutes at the "Pressure" mode. When the cooking time ends, release the remaining pressure and open the pressure cooker lid. Serve the chicken piccata immediately.

Nutrition Values Per Serving:

calories 257, fat 16.3, fiber 0.8, carbs 1.6, protein 25.2

Sour Cream Chicken Liver

Prepping time: 10 minutes

Cooking time: 18 minutes

Servings: 7

Ingredients:

- 1 pound chicken livers
- 1 onion
- 1 teaspoon garlic powder
- 1 tablespoon cilantro

- ¼ cup dill
- 1 teaspoon olive oil
- 1 cup cream
- ¼ cup cream cheese
- 1 teaspoon salt
- 1 teaspoon ground white pepper

Preparation:

Chop the chicken livers roughly and place them into the pressure cooker. Set the pressure cooker to "Sauté" mode. Sprinkle the liver with the olive oil and sauté it for 3 minutes, stirring frequently. Combine the sour cream and cream cheese together in a mixing bowl. Sprinkle the mixture with the cilantro, garlic powder, salt, and ground black pepper and stir well. Pour the sour cream mixture into the pressure cooker and stir well. Close the pressure cooker lid and cook the dish on "Sear/Sauté" mode for 15 minutes. When the dish is cooked, let it rest briefly and serve.

Nutrition Values Per Serving:

calories 239, fat 18.2, fiber 0, carbs 8.22, protein 11

Crunchy Oregano Drumsticks

Prepping time: 10 minutes

Cooking time: 11 minutes

Servings: 8

Ingredients:

- 1 cup pork rind
- 1 tablespoon salt
- 1 tablespoon paprika
- 1 teaspoon ground black pepper
- 1 teaspoon cayenne pepper
- 1 teaspoon oregano
- ½ cup olive oil
- 1 tablespoon minced garlic
- 1 pound chicken drumsticks
- ½ cup cream
- 1 cup cream cheese

Preparation:

Combine the pork rind, salt, paprika, ground black pepper, cayenne pepper, oregano, and minced garlic in a mixing bowl and stir well. Combine the cream and cream cheese together in separate mixing bowl. Whisk the mixture until smooth. Pour the olive oil into the pressure cooker and preheat it at the "Sauté" mode for 3 minutes. Dip the drumsticks in the cream cheese mixture and Dip them in the pork rind mixture. Transfer the chicken into the pressure cooker and cook for 8 minutes until you golden brown. When the drumsticks are cooked, remove them from the pressure cooker, and drain them on a paper towel to remove excess oil before serving.

Nutrition Values Per Serving:

calories 421, fat 33.2, fiber 0.6, carbs 2.5, protein 29.4

Chicken with Veggies

Prepping time: 20 mins

Cooking Time: 8 hours 40 minutes

Servings: 8

Ingredients:

- 2 pounds skinless, boneless chicken breast tenders
- 1 large onion, chopped
- 2 cups asparagus, trimmed and cut into 2-inch pieces
- 1 tablespoon fresh thyme, chopped
- 1 teaspoon garlic powder
- Salt and ground black pepper, as required
- 4 medium zucchinis, spiralized with blade C
- 1 cup sour cream
- 1 cup cheddar cheese, shredded

Preparation:

1. In the pot of Ninja Foodi, add the chicken, onion, asparagus, thyme, garlic powder, salt, and black pepper and mix well.
2. Close the Ninja Foodi with a crisping lid and select "Slow Cooker."
3. Set on "Low" for 8 hours.
4. Press "Start/Stop" to begin cooking.
5. Open the lid and
6. Place the zucchini noodles over the chicken mixture and top with cheese and cream.
7. Close the Ninja Foodi with a crisping lid and select "Slow Cooker."
8. Set on "Low" for 30-40 minutes.
9. Press "Start/Stop" to begin cooking.
10. Open the lid and stir the mixture well.
11. Serve hot.

Nutrition Values Per Serving:

Calories: 292, Fat: 15 g, Saturated Fat: 8.3 g, Trans Fat: 6.7 g, Carbohydrates: 8.2 g, Fiber 2.3 g, Sodium 174 mg, Protein: 32 g

Indian Chicken

Prepping time: 10 minutes

Cooking time: 30 minutes

Servings: 8

Ingredients:

- 1 tablespoon curry paste

- 1 tablespoon lemongrass paste
- ½ cup fresh thyme
- 2 pound of chicken breasts
- 1 cup almond milk
- ½ cup cream
- 1 teaspoon salt
- 1 teaspoon cilantro
- 1 tablespoon olive oil

Preparation:

Wash the thyme and chop it. Combine the almond milk with the curry paste and lemongrass paste. Stir the mixture until everything is dissolved. Add cilantro, salt, and cream. Add the chopped thyme and chicken breasts. Let the chicken sit for 10 minutes. Set the pressure cooker to "Sear/Sauté" mode. Transfer the chicken mixture into the pressure cooker and close the lid. Cook the chicken for 30 minutes. When the cooking time ends, remove the dish from the pressure cooker and remove the chicken from the cream mixture, slice it and serve.

Nutrition Values Per Serving:

calories 261, fat 15.6, fiber 1, carbs 4.77, protein 25

Spicy Whole Turkey

Prepping time: 15 mins

Cooking Time: 8 hours 5 minutes

Servings: 14

Ingredients:

For Spice Rub:
- 2 teaspoons dried thyme, crushed
- 2 teaspoons ground cumin
- 2 teaspoons paprika
- 2 teaspoons salt
- 1 teaspoon ground white pepper
- 1 teaspoon ground black pepper

For Turkey:
- 1 (8-pound) whole turkey, necks, and giblets removed
- 4 garlic cloves, peeled and smashed
- ½ of medium onion, chopped
- 2 carrots, scrubbed and cut into thirds
- 2 celery stalks, cut into thirds
- 1 whole lemon, quartered

Preparation:
1. For the spice rub: in a bowl, mix all ingredients. Keep aside.
2. Rinse turkey well, and with a paper towel, pat dries completely.

3. Fold back the wings of the turkey.

4. Rub smashed garlic over outside of turkey evenly.

5. Rub inside and outside of turkey with spice rub generously.

6. Place lemon quarters in the cavity of the turkey.

7. Tie the legs of the turkey with kitchen twine.

8. In the pot of a Ninja Foodi, place the onion, carrots, celery, and 3 garlic cloves.

9. Arrange turkey over vegetables.

10. Close the Ninja Foodi with crisping lid and select "Slow Cooker".

11. Set on "High" for 6-8 hours.

12. Press "Start/Stop" to begin cooking.

13. Now, close the Ninja Foodi with crisping lid and select "Broil" for 5 minutes.

14. Press "Start/Stop" to begin cooking.

15. Open the lid and place the turkey onto a platter for about 25-30 minutes before slicing.

16. Cut into desired sized pieces and serve alongside vegetables.

Nutrition Values Per Serving:

Calories: 403, Fat: 18.6 g, Saturated Fat: 5.8 g, Trans Fat: 12.8 g, Carbohydrates: 2.2 g, Fiber 0.6 g, Sodium 1175 mg, Protein: 48.9 g

Chapter 5-Fish and Seafood Recipes

Sweet and Sour Fish

Prepping time: 10 minutes

Cooking time: 6 minutes

Servings: 4

Ingredients:

- 2 drops liquid stevia
- 1/4 cup butter
- 1 pound fish chunks
- 1 tablespoon vinegar
- Salt and pepper to taste

Preparation:

1. Set your Ninja Foodi to Saute mode and add butter, let it melt
2. Add fish chunks and Saute for 3 minutes. Add stevia, salt, and pepper, stir
3. Lock Crisping Lid and cook on "Air Crisp" mode for 3 minutes at 360 degrees F
4. Serve once done and enjoy!

Nutrition Values Per Serving:

Calories: 274, Fat: 15g, Carbohydrates: 2g, Protein: 33g

Alaskan Cod Divine

Prepping time: 10 minutes

Cooking time: 5-10 minutes

Servings: 4

Ingredients:

- 1 large fillet, Alaskan Cod (Frozen)
- 1 cup cherry tomatoes
- Salt and pepper to taste
- Seasoning as you need
- 2 tablespoons butter
- Olive oil as needed

Preparation:

1. Take an ovenproof dish small enough to fit inside your pot
2. Add tomatoes to the dish, cut large fish fillet into 2-3 serving pieces and lay them on top of tomatoes. Season with salt, pepper, and your seasoning
3. Top each fillet with 1 tablespoon butter and drizzle olive oil
4. Add 1 cup of water to the pot.Place trivet to the Ninja Foodi and place dish on the trivet
5. Lock lid and cook on HIGH pressure for 9 minutes.Release pressure naturally over 10 minutes

6. Serve and enjoy!

Nutrition Values Per Serving:

Calories: 449, Fat: 32g, Carbohydrates: 11g, Protein: 25g

Fish Nuggets

Prepping Time: 30 minutes

Servings: 4

Ingredients:

- 1 lb. cod fillet, sliced into 8 pieces
- Salt and pepper to taste
- 1/2 cup flour
- 1 tablespoon egg with 1 teaspoon water
- 1 cup bread crumbs
- 1 tablespoon vegetable oil

Preparation:

1. Season the fish with salt and pepper. Cover with the flour.
2. Dip the fish in the egg wash and into the bread crumbs.
3. Place the fish nuggets in the Ninja Foodi basket. Set it to air crisp function.
4. Seal with the crisping lid. Cook at 360 degrees for 15 minutes.

Serving Suggestion: Serve with lemon honey tartar sauce.

Tip: Add dried dill or garlic powder to the seasoning to make it tastier.

Nutritional Information Per Serving:

Calories 234, Total Fat 5.4g, Saturated Fat 1g, Cholesterol 25mg, Sodium 229mg, Total Carbohydrate 31.4g, Dietary Fiber 1.7g, Total Sugars 1.7g, Protein 14.1g, Potassium 70mg

Pepper and Salt Shrimp

Prepping Time: 20 minutes

Servings: 4

Ingredients:

- 2 teaspoons peppercorns
- 1 teaspoon salt
- 1 teaspoons sugar
- 1 lb. shrimp
- 3 tablespoons rice flour
- 2 tablespoons oil

Preparation:

1. Set the Ninja Foodi to sauté. Roast the peppercorns for 1 minute. Let them cool.
2. Crush the peppercorns and add the salt and sugar.
3. Coat the shrimp with this mixture and then with flour.

4. Sprinkle oil on the Ninja Foodi basket. Place the shrimp on top.

5. Cook at 350 degrees for 10 minutes, flipping halfway through.

Nutritional Information Per Serving:

Calories 228, Total Fat 8.9g, Saturated Fat 1.5g, Cholesterol 239mg, Sodium 859mg, Total Carbohydrate 9.3g, Dietary Fiber 0.5g, Total Sugars 1g, Protein 26.4g, Potassium 211mg

Amazing Panko Cod

Prepping time: 5 minutes

Cooking time: 15 minutes

Serving: 6

Ingredients:

- 2 uncooked cod fillets, 6 ounces each
- 3 teaspoons kosher salt
- 3/4 cup panko bread crumbs
- 2 tablespoons butter, melted
- 1/4 cup fresh parsley, minced
- 1 lemon. Zested and juiced

Preparation:

1. Pre-heat your Ninja Foodi at 390 degrees F and place Air Crisper basket inside

2. Season cod and salt

3. Take a bowl and add bread crumbs, parsley, lemon juice, zest, butter, and mix well

4. Coat fillets with the bread crumbs mixture and place fillets in your Air Crisping basket

5. Lock Air Crisping lid and cook on Air Crisp mode for 15 minutes at 360 degrees F

6. Serve and enjoy!

Nutrition Values Per Serving:

Calories: 554, Fat: 24g, Carbohydrates: 5g, Protein: 37g

Tasty Carb Soup

Prepping time: 5 minutes

Cooking time: 6-7 hours

Servings: 4

Ingredients:

- 1 cup crab meat, cubed
- 1 tablespoon garlic, minced
- Salt as needed
- Red chili flakes as needed
- 3 cups vegetable broth
- 1 teaspoon salt

Preparation:

1. Coat the crab cubes in lime juice and let them sit for a while
2. Add the all ingredients (including marinated crab meat) to your Ninja Foodi and lock lid
3. Cook on SLOW COOK MODE (MEDIUM) for 3 hours
4. Let it sit for a while
5. Unlock lid and set to Saute mode, simmer the soup for 5 minutes more on LOW
6. Stir and check to season. Enjoy!

Nutrition Values Per Serving:

Calories: 201, Fat: 11g, Carbohydrates: 12g, Protein: 13g

Salmon and Kale Delight

Prepping time: 10 minutes

Cooking time: 5 minutes

Servings: 4

Ingredients:

- 1 lemon, juiced
- 2 salmon fillets
- 1/4 cup extra virgin olive oil
- 1 teaspoon Dijon mustard
- 4 cups kale, thinly sliced, ribs removed
- 1 teaspoon salt
- 1 avocado, diced
- 1 cup pomegranate seeds
- 1 cup walnuts, toasted
- 1 cup goat parmesan cheese, shredded

Preparation:

1. Season salmon with salt and keep it on the side. Place a trivet in your Ninja Foodi
2. Place salmon over the trivet. Lock lid and cook on HIGH pressure for 15 minutes
3. Release pressure naturally over 10 minutes. Transfer salmon to a serving platter
4. Take a bowl and add kale, season with salt
5. Take another bowl and make the dressing by adding lemon juice, Dijon mustard, olive oil, and red wine vinegar. Season kale with dressing and add diced avocado, pomegranate seeds, walnuts and cheese. Toss and serve with the fish. Enjoy!

Nutrition Values Per Serving:

Calories: 234, Fat: 14g, Carbohydrates: 12g, Protein: 16g

Cod Fish

Prepping Time: 30 minutes

Servings: 4

Ingredients:

- 4 cod fish fillets
- Salt and sugar to taste
- 1 teaspoon sesame oil
- 250 ml water
- 5 tablespoons light soy sauce
- 1 teaspoon dark soy sauce
- 3 tablespoons oil
- 5 slices ginger

Preparation:

1. Pat the cod fish fillets dry.
2. Season with the salt, sugar and sesame oil. Marinate for 15 minutes.
3. Set the Ninja Foodi to air crisp.
4. Put the fish on top of the basket. Cook at 350 degrees F for 3 minutes.
5. Flip and cook for 2 minutes. Take the fish out and set aside.
6. Put the rest of the ingredients in the pot.
7. Set it to sauté. Simmer and pour over the fish before serving.

Serving Suggestion: Sprinkle top with chopped green onion.

Nutritional Information Per Serving:

Calories 303, Total Fat 13.1g, Saturated Fat 1.9g, Cholesterol 99mg, Sodium 144mg, Total Carbohydrate 2.9g, Dietary Fiber 0.5g, Total Sugars 0.1g, Protein 41.5g, Potassium 494mg

Lemon Garlic Shrimp

Prepping Time: 40 minutes

Servings: 4

Ingredients:

- 1 lb. shrimp, peeled and deveined
- 1 tablespoon olive oil
- 4 cloves garlic, minced
- 1 tablespoon lemon juice
- Salt to taste

Preparation:

1. Mix the olive oil, salt, lemon juice and garlic.Toss shrimp in the mixture.
2. Marinate for 15 minutes. Place the shrimp in the Ninja Foodi basket.
3. Seal the crisping lid. Select the air crisp setting.
4. Cook at 350 degrees for 8 minutes. Flip and cook for 2 more minutes.

Nutritional Information Per Serving:

Calories 170, Total Fat 5.5g, Saturated Fat 1.1g, Cholesterol 239mg, Sodium 317mg, Total Carbohydrate 2.8g, Dietary Fiber 0.1g, Total Sugars 0.1g, Protein 26.1g, Potassium 209mg

Garlic and Lemon Prawn Delight

Prepping time: 5 minutes

Cooking time: 5 minutes

Servings: 4

Ingredients:

- 2 tablespoons olive oil
- 1 pound prawns
- 2 tablespoons garlic, minced
- 2/3 cup fish stock
- 1 tablespoon butter
- 2 tablespoons lemon juice
- 1 tablespoon lemon zest
- Salt and pepper to taste

Preparation:

1. Set your Ninja Foodi to Saute mode and add butter and oil, let it heat up
2. Stir in remaining ingredients. Lock lid and cook on LOW pressure for 5 minutes
3. Quick release pressure. Serve and enjoy!

Nutrition Values Per Serving:

Calories: 236, Fat: 12g, Carbohydrates: 2g, Protein: 27g

Air Fried Scallops

Prepping time: 5 minutes

Cooking time: 5 minutes

Servings: 4

Ingredients:

- 12 scallops
- 3 tablespoons olive oil
- Salt and pepper to taste

Preparation:

1. Gently rub scallops with salt, pepper, and oil
2. Transfer to your Ninja Foodi's insert, and place the insert in your Foodi
3. Lock Air Crisping lid and cook for 4 minutes at 390 degrees F
4. Half through, make sure to give them a nice flip and keep cooking. Serve warm and enjoy!

Nutrition Values Per Serving:

Calories: 372, Fat: 11g, Carbohydrates: 0.9g, Protein: 63g

Heartfelt Sesame Fish

Prepping time: 8 minutes

Cooking time: 8 minutes

Servings: 4

Ingredients:

- 1 and 1/2 pound salmon fillet
- 1 teaspoon sesame seeds
- 1 teaspoon butter, melted
- 1/2 teaspoon salt
- 1 tablespoon apple cider vinegar
- 1/4 teaspoon rosemary, dried

Preparation:

1. Take apple cider vinegar and spray it to the salmon fillets
2. Then add dried rosemary, sesame seeds, butter and salt
3. Mix them well. Take butter sauce and brush the salmon properly
4. Place the salmon on the rack and lower the air fryer lid. Set the air fryer mode
5. Cook the fish for 8 minutes at 360 F. Serve hot and enjoy!

Nutrition Values Per Serving:

Calories: 239, Fat: 11.2g, Carbohydrates: 0.3g, Protein: 33.1g

Pepper and Lemon Salmon Delight

Prepping time: 5 minutes

Cooking time: 6 minutes

Servings: 4

Ingredients:

- 3/4 cup of water
- Sprigs of parsley, basil, tarragon
- 1 pound salmon, skin on
- 3 teaspoons ghee
- 3/4 teaspoon salt
- 1/2 teaspoon pepper
- 1/2 lemon, sliced
- 1 red bell pepper, julienned
- 1 carrot, julienned

Preparation:

1. Set your Ninja Foodi to Saute mode and add water and herbs
2. Place a steamer rack and add the salmon. Drizzle ghee on top of the salmon
3. Season with pepper and salt. Cover lemon slices on top

4. Lock up the lid and cook on HIGH pressure for 3 minutes

5. Release the pressure naturally over 10 minutes

6. Transfer the salmon to a platter. Add veggies to your pot and set the pot to Saute mode

7. Cook for 1-2 minutes. Serve the cooked vegetables with salmon. Enjoy!

Nutrition Values Per Serving:

Calories: 464, Fat: 34g, Carbohydrates: 3g, Protein: 34g

Sweet Tuna Patties

Prepping Time: 30 minutes

Servings: 2

Ingredients:

- 2 cans tuna flakes
- 1/2 tablespoon almond flour
- 1 teaspoon dried dill
- 1 tablespoon mayo
- 1/2 teaspoon onion powder
- 1 teaspoon garlic powder
- Salt and pepper to taste
- 1 tablespoon lemon juice

Preparation:

1. Mix all the ingredients in a bowl. Form patties. Set the tuna patties on the Ninja Foodi basket. Seal the crisping lid. Set it to air crisp.

2. Cook at 400 degrees for 10 minutes. Flip and cook for 5 more minutes.

Nutritional Information Per Serving:

Calories 141, Total Fat 6.4g, Saturated Fat 0.7g, Cholesterol 17mg, Sodium 148mg, Total Carbohydrate 5.2g, Dietary Fiber 1g, Total Sugars 1.2g, Protein 17g, Potassium 48mg

The Rich Guy Lobster and Butter

Prepping time: 15 minutes

Cooking time: 20 minutes

Servings: 4

Ingredients:

- 6 Lobster Tails
- 4 garlic cloves,
- 1/4 cup butter

Preparation:

1. Preheat the Ninja Foodi to 400 degrees F at first

2. Open the lobster tails gently by using kitchen scissors

3. Remove the lobster meat gently from the shells but keep it inside the shells

4. Take a plate and place it

5. Add some butter in a pan and allow it melt

6. Put some garlic cloves in it and heat it over medium-low heat

7. Pour the garlic butter mixture all over the lobster tail meat

8. Let the fryer to broil the lobster at 130 degrees F

9. Remove the lobster meat from Ninja Foodi and set aside

10. Use a fork to pull out the lobster meat from the shells entirely

11. Pour some garlic butter over it if needed. Serve and enjoy!

Nutrition Values Per Serving:

Calories: 160, Fat: 1g, Carbohydrates: 1g, Protein: 20g

Breathtaking Cod Fillets

Prepping time: 10 minutes

Cooking time: 5-10 minutes

Servings: 4

Ingredients:

*   1 pound frozen cod fish fillets
*   2 garlic cloves, halved
*   1 cup chicken broth
*   1/2 cup packed parsley
*   2 tablespoons oregano
*   2 tablespoons almonds, sliced½ teaspoon paprika

Preparation:

1. Take the fish out of the freezer and let it defrost

2. Take a food processor and stir in garlic, oregano, parsley, paprika, 1 tablespoon almond and process. Set your Ninja Foodi to "SAUTE" mode and add olive oil, let it heat up

3. Add remaining almonds and toast, transfer to a towel. Pour broth in a pot and add herb mixture

4. Cut fish into 4 pieces and place in a steamer basket, transfer steamer basket to the pot

5. Lock lid and cook on HIGH pressure for 3 minutes. Quick release pressure once has done

6. Serve steamed fish by pouring over the sauce.Enjoy!

Nutrition Values Per Serving:

Calories: 246, Fat: 10g, Carbohydrates: 8g, Protein: 15g

Awesome Cherry Tomato Mackerel

Prepping time: 5 minutes

Cooking time: 7 minutes

Servings: 4

Ingredients:

*   4 Mackerel fillets

- 1/4 teaspoon onion powder
- 1/4 teaspoon lemon powder
- 1/4 teaspoon garlic powder
- 1/2 teaspoon salt
- 2 cups cherry tomatoes
- 3 tablespoons melted butter
- 1 and 1/2 cups of water
- 1 tablespoon black olives

Preparation:

1. Grease baking dish and arrange cherry tomatoes at the bottom of the dish
2. Top with fillets sprinkle all spices. Drizzle melted butter over
3. Add water to your Ninja Foodi
4. Lower rack in Ninja Foodi and place baking dish on top of the rack
5. Lock lid and cook on LOW pressure for 7 minutes. Quick release pressure. Serve and enjoy!

Nutrition Values Per Serving:

Calories: 325, Fat: 24g, Carbohydrates: 2g, Protein: 21g

Awesome Sock-Eye Salmon

Prepping time: 5 minutes

Cooking time: 5 minutes

Servings: 4

Ingredients:

- 4 sockeye salmon fillets
- 1 teaspoon Dijon mustard
- 1/4 teaspoon garlic, minced
- 1/4 teaspoon onion powder
- 1/4 teaspoon lemon pepper
- 1/2 teaspoon garlic powder
- 1/4 teaspoon salt
- 2 tablespoons olive oil
- 1 and 1/2 cup of water

Preparation:

1. Take a bowl and add mustard, lemon juice, onion powder, lemon pepper, garlic powder, salt, olive oil. Brush spice mix over salmon
2. Add water to Instant Pot. Place rack and place salmon fillets on rack
3. Lock lid and cook on LOW pressure for 7 minutes
4. Quick release pressure. Serve and enjoy!

Nutrition Values Per Serving:

Calories: 353, Fat: 25g, Carbohydrates: 0.6g, Protein: 40g

Delicious Salmon Paprika

Prepping time: 5 minutes

Cooking time: 7 minutes

Servings: 4

Ingredients:

- 2 wild caught salmon fillets, 1 to 1 and ½ inches thick
- 2 teaspoons avocado oil
- 2 teaspoons paprika
- Salt and pepper to taste
- Green herbs to garnish

Preparation:

1. Season salmon fillets with salt, pepper, paprika, and olive oil
2. Place Crisping basket in your Ninja Foodi, and pre-heat your Ninja Foodi at 390 degrees F
3. Place insert insider your Foodi and place the fillet in the insert, lock Air Crisping lid and cook for 7 minutes. Once done, serve the fish with herbs on top. Enjoy!

Nutrition Values Per Serving:

Calories: 249, Fat: 11g, Carbohydrates: 1.8g, Protein: 35g

Packets of Lemon and Dill Cod

Prepping time: 10 minutes

Cooking time: 5-10 minutes

Servings: 4

Ingredients:

- 2 tilapia cod fillets
- Salt, pepper and garlic powder to taste
- 2 sprigs fresh dill
- 4 slices lemon
- 2 tablespoons butter

Preparation:

1. Layout 2 large squares of parchment paper
2. Place fillet in center of each parchment square and season with salt, pepper and garlic powder
3. On each fillet, place 1 sprig of dill, 2 lemon slices, 1 tablespoon butter
4. Place trivet at the bottom of your Ninja Foodi. Add 1 cup water into the pot
5. Close parchment paper around fillets and fold to make a nice seal
6. Place both packets in your pot. Lock lid and cook on HIGH pressure for 5 minutes
7. Quick release pressure. Serve and enjoy!

Nutrition Values Per Serving:

Calories: 259, Fat: 11g, Carbohydrates: 8g, Protein: 20g

Fresh Steamed Salmon

Prepping time: 5 minutes

Cooking time: 5 minutes

Servings: 4

Ingredients:

- 2 salmon fillets
- 1/4 cup onion, chopped
- 2 stalks green onion stalks, chopped
- 1 whole egg
- Almond meal
- Salt and pepper to taste
- 2 tablespoons olive oil

Preparation:

1. Add a cup of water to your Ninja Foodi and place a steamer rack on top
2. Place the fish. Season the fish with salt and pepper and lock up the lid
3. Cook on HIGH pressure for 3 minutes. Once done, quick release the pressure
4. Remove the fish and allow it to cool
5. Break the fillets into a bowl and add egg, yellow and green onions
6. Add 1/2 a cup of almond meal and mix with your hand. Divide the mixture into patties
7. Take a large skillet and place it over medium heat. Add oil and cook the patties.Enjoy!

Nutrition Values Per Serving:

Calories: 238, Fat: 15g, Carbohydrates: 1g, Protein: 23g

Air Fried Scampi

Prepping time: 5 minutes

Cooking time: 5 minutes

Servings: 4

Ingredients:

- 4 tablespoons butter
- 1 tablespoon lemon juice
- 1 tablespoon garlic, minced
- 2 teaspoons red pepper flakes
- 1 tablespoon chives, chopped
- 1 tablespoon basil leaves, minced
- 2 tablespoons chicken stock
- 1 pound defrosted shrimp

Preparation:

1. Set your Foodi to Saute mode and add butter, let the butter melt and add red pepper flakes and garlic, Saute for 2 minutes
2. Transfer garlic to crisping basket, add remaining ingredients (including shrimp) to the basket
3. Return basket back to the Ninja Foodi and lock the Air Crisping lid, cook for 5 minutes at 390 degrees F. Once done, serve with a garnish of fresh basil

Nutrition Values Per Serving:

Calories: 372, Fat: 11g, Carbohydrates: 0.9g, Protein: 63g

Ranch Warm Fillets

Prepping time: 5 minutes

Cooking time: 13 minutes

Servings: 4

Ingredients:

- 1/4 cup panko
- 1/2 packet ranch dressing mix powder
- 1 and 1/4 tablespoons vegetable oil
- 1 egg beaten
- 2 tilapia fillets
- A garnish of herbs and chilies

Preparation:

1. Pre-heat your Ninja Foodi with the Crisping Basket inside at 350 degrees F
2. Take a bowl and mix in ranch dressing and panko
3. Beat eggs in a shallow bowl and keep it on the side
4. Dip fillets in the eggs, then in the panko mix
5. Place fillets in your Ninja Foodi's insert and transfer insert to Ninja Foodi
6. Lock Air Crisping Lid and Air Crisp for 13 minutes at 350 degrees F
7. Garnish with chilies and herbs. Enjoy!

Nutrition Values Per Serving:

Calories: 301, Fat: 12g, Carbohydrates: 1.5g, Protein: 28g

Buttered Up Scallops

Prepping time: 10 minutes

Cooking time: 5 minutes

Servings: 4

Ingredients:

- 4 garlic cloves, minced
- 4 tablespoons rosemary, chopped
- 2 pounds sea scallops
- 12 cup butter
- Salt and pepper to taste

Preparation:

1. Set your Ninja Foodi to Saute mode and add butter, rosemary, and garlic
2. Saute for 1 minute. Add scallops, salt, and pepper
3. Saute for 2 minutes. Lock Crisping lid and Crisp for 3 minutes at 350 degrees F. Serve and enjoy!

Nutrition Values Per Serving:

Calories: 279, Fat: 16g, Carbohydrates: 5g, Protein: 25g

Chapter 6-Vegan and Vegetarian Recipes

Mixed Vegetable Curry

Prepping time: 10 minutes

Cooking time: 3 minutes

Serving: 6

Ingredients:

- 3 cups leeks, sliced
- 6 cups rainbow chard, stems and leaves, chopped
- 1 cup celery, chopped
- 2 tablespoons garlic, minced
- 1 teaspoon dried oregano
- 1 teaspoon salt
- 2 teaspoons fresh ground black pepper
- 3 cups chicken broth
- 2 cups yellow summer squash, sliced into 1/ inch slices
- ¼ cup fresh parsley, chopped
- ¾ cup heavy whip cream
- 4-6 tablespoons parmesan cheese, grated

Preparation:

1. Add leeks, chard, celery, 1 tablespoon garlic, oregano, salt, pepper and broth to your Ninja Foodi
2. Lock lid and cook on HIGH pressure for 3 minutes. Quick release pressure
3. Open the lid and add more broth, set your pot to Saute mode and adjust heat to HIGH
4. Add yellow squash, parsley and remaining 1 tablespoon garlic
5. Let it cook for 2-3 minutes until the squash is soft. Stir in cream and sprinkle parmesan
6. Serve and enjoy!

Nutrition Values Per Serving:

Calories: 210, Fat: 14g, Carbohydrates: 10g, Protein: 10g

A Mishmash Cauliflower Mash

Prepping time: 10 minutes

Cooking time: 5 minutes

Servings: 3

Ingredients:

- 1 tablespoon butter, soft
- ½ cup feta cheese
- Salt and pepper to taste

- 1 large head cauliflower, chopped into large pieces
- 1 garlic cloves, minced
- 2 teaspoons fresh chives, minced

Preparation:

1. Add water to your Ninja Foodi and place steamer basket
2. Add cauliflower pieces and lock lid, cook on HIGH pressure for 5 minutes
3. Quick release pressure. Open the lid and use an immersion blender to mash the cauliflower
4. Blend until you have a nice consistency. Enjoy!

Nutrition Values Per Serving:

Calories: 124, Fat: 10g, Carbohydrates: 5g, Protein: 5g

Beet Borscht

Prepping time: 5 minutes

Cooking time: 45 minutes

Serving: 6

Ingredients:

- 8 cups beets
- ½ cup celery, diced
- ½ cup carrots, diced
- 2 garlic cloves, diced
- 1 medium onion, diced
- 3 cups cabbage, shredded
- 6 cups beef stock
- 1 bay leaf
- 1 tablespoon salt
- ½ tablespoon thyme
- ¼ cup fresh dill, chopped
- ½ cup of coconut yogurt

Preparation:

1. Add the washed beets to a steamer in the Ninja Foodi
2. Add 1 cup of water. Steam for 7 minutes
3. Perform a quick release and drop into an ice bath
4. Carefully peel off the skin and dice the beets
5. Transfer the diced beets, celery, carrots, onion, garlic, cabbage, stock, bay leaf, thyme and salt to your Instant Pot. Lock up the lid and set the pot to SOUP mode, cook for 45 minutes
6. Release the pressure naturally. Transfer to bowls and top with a dollop of dairy-free yogurt
7. Enjoy with a garnish of fresh dill!

Nutrition Values Per Serving:

Calories: 625, Fats: 46g, Carbs:19g, Protein:90g

Lemon Artichokes

Prepping time: 10 minutes

Cooking time: 5 hours

Servings: 4

Ingredients:

- 5 large artichokes
- 1 teaspoon of sea salt
- 2 stalks celery, sliced
- 2 large carrots, cut into matchsticks
- Juice from ½ a lemon
- ¼ teaspoon black pepper
- 1 teaspoon dried thyme
- 1 tablespoon dried rosemary
- Lemon wedges for garnish

Preparation:

1. Remove the stalk from your artichokes and remove the tough outer shell
2. Transfer the chokes to your Ninja Foodi and add 2 cups of boiling water
3. Add celery, lemon juice, salt, carrots, black pepper, thyme, rosemary
4. Cook on Slow Cook mode (HIGH) for 4-5 hours
5. Serve the artichokes with lemon wedges. Serve and enjoy!

Nutrition Values Per Serving:

Calories: 205, Fat: 2g, Carbohydrates: 12g, Protein: 34g

Fresh Onion Soup

Prepping time: 5 minutes

Cooking time: 10-15 minutes

Servings: 4

Ingredients:

- 2 tablespoons avocado oil
- 8 cups yellow onion
- 1 tablespoon balsamic vinegar
- 6 cups of pork stock
- 1 teaspoon salt
- 2 bay leaves
- 2 large sprigs, fresh thyme

Preparation:

1. Cut up the onion in half through the root
2. Peel them and slice into thin half moons

3. Set the pot to Saute mode and add oil, one the oil is hot and add onions
4. Cook for about 15 minutes
5. Add balsamic vinegar and scrape any fond from the bottom
6. Add stock, bay leaves, salt, and thyme
7. Lock up the lid and cook on HIGH pressure for 10 minutes
8. Release the pressure naturally
9. Discard the bay leaf and thyme stems
10. Blend the soup using an immersion blender and serve!

Nutrition Values Per Serving:

Calories: 454, Fat: 31g, Carbohydrates: 7g, Protein: 27g

Rice Cauliflower

Prepping time: 10 minutes

Cooking time: 15 minutes

Servings: 4

Ingredients:

- 1 large cauliflower head
- 2 tablespoons olive oil
- ¼ teaspoon salt
- ½ teaspoon dried parsley
- ½ teaspoon cumin
- ¼ teaspoon turmeric
- ¼ teaspoon paprika
- Fresh cilantro
- Lime wedges

Preparation:

1. Wash the cauliflower well and trim the leaves
2. Place a steamer rack on top of the pot and transfer the florets to the rack
3. Add 1 cup of water into the Ninja Foodi.Lock up the lid and cook on HIGH pressure for 1 minute
4. Once done, do a quick release.Transfer the flower to a serving platter
5. Set your pot to Saute mode and add oil, allow the oil to heat up
6. Add flowers back to the pot and cook, making sure to break them using a potato masher
7. Add spices and season with a bit of salt. Give a nice stir and squeeze a bit of lime
8. Serve and enjoy!

Nutrition Values Per Serving:

Calories: 169, Fat: 14g, Carbohydrates: 8g, Protein: 3g

Vegetable Platter

Prepping time: 5 minutes

Cooking time: 3 hours 5 minutes

Serving: 6

Ingredients:

- 1 cup grape tomatoes
- 2 cups okra
- 1 cup mushrooms
- 2 cups yellow bell peppers
- 1 and ½ cup red onions
- 2 and ½ cups zucchini
- ½ cup olive oil
- ½ cup balsamic vinegar
- 1 tablespoon fresh thyme, chopped
- 2 tablespoons fresh basil, chopped

Preparation:

1. Slice and chop okra, onions, tomatoes, zucchini, mushrooms
2. Add veggies to a large container and mix
3. Take another dish and add oil and vinegar, mix in thyme and basil
4. Toss the veggies into Ninja Foodi and pour marinade. Stir well
5. Close lid and cook on 3 hours on SLOW COOK MOD (HIGH), making sure to stir after every hour

Nutrition Values Per Serving:

Calories: 233, Fat: 18g, Carbohydrates: 14g, Protein: 3g

Green Beans Platter

Prepping time: 10 minutes

Cooking time: 5 minutes

Serving: 6

Ingredients:

- 2-3 pounds fresh green beans
- 2 tablespoons butter
- 1 garlic clove, minced
- Salt and pepper to taste
- 1 and ½ cups of water

Preparation:

1. Add listed ingredients to Ninja Foodi. Lock lid and cook on HIGH pressure for 5 minutes
2. Quick release pressure

Nutrition Values Per Serving:

Calories: 87, Fat: 6g, Carbohydrates: 5g, Protein: 3g

Zucchini Pesto Meal

Prepping time: 10 minutes

Cooking time: 10 minutes

Servings: 4

Ingredients:

- 1 tablespoon olive oil
- 1 onion, chopped
- 2 and ½ pound roughly chopped zucchini
- ½ cup of water
- 1 and ½ teaspoon salt
- 1 bunch basil leaves
- 2 garlic cloves, minced
- 1 tablespoon extra-virgin olive oil
- Zucchini for making zoodles

Preparation:

1. Set the Ninja Foodi to Saute mode and add olive oil
2. Once the oil is hot, add onion and Saute for 4 minutes
3. Add zucchini, water, and salt. Lock up the lid and cook on HIGH pressure for 3 minutes
4. Release the pressure naturally. Add basil, garlic, and leaves
5. Use an immersion blender to blend everything well until you have a sauce-like consistency
6. Take the extra zucchini and pass them through a Spiralizer to get noodle like shapes
7. Toss the Zoodles with sauce and enjoy!

Nutrition Values Per Serving:

Calories: 71, Fat: 4g, Carbohydrates: 6g, Protein: 3g

Red Cabbage

Prepping time: 10 minutes

Cooking time: 10 minutes

Serving: 6

Ingredients:

- 6 cups red cabbage, chopped
- 1 tablespoon apple cider vinegar
- ½ cup Keto-Friendly applesauce
- 1 cup of water
- 3 garlic cloves, minced
- 1 small onion, chopped
- 1 tablespoon olive oil

- Salt and pepper to taste

Preparation:

1. Add olive oil to Ninja Foodi
2. Set it to Saute mode and let it heat up, add onion and garlic and Saute for 2 minutes
3. Add remaining ingredients and stir. Lock lid and cook on HIGH pressure for 10 minutes
4. Quick release pressure. Stir well and serve. Enjoy!

Nutrition Values Per Serving:

Calories: 81, Fat: 6g, Carbohydrates: 4g, Protein: 2g

Mushroom Stroganoff

Prepping time: 5 minutes

Cooking time: 10 minutes

Serving: 6

Ingredients:

- ¼ cup unsalted butter, cubed
- 1 pound cremini mushrooms, halved
- 1 large onion, halved
- 4 garlic cloves, minced
- 2 cups vegetable broth
- ½ teaspoon salt
- ¼ teaspoon fresh black pepper
- 1 and ½ cups sour cream
- ¼ cup fresh flat-leaf parsley, chopped
- 1 cup grated parmesan cheese

Preparation:

1. Add butter, mushrooms, onion, garlic, vegetable broth, salt, pepper, and paprika
2. Gently stir and lock lid. Cook on HIGH pressure for 5 minutes
3. Release pressure naturally over 10 minutes
4. Serve by stirring in sour cream and with a garnish of parsley and parmesan cheese. Enjoy!

Nutrition Values Per Serving:

Calories: 453, Fat: 37g, Carbohydrates: 11g, Protein: 19g

Garlic and Ginger Red Cabbage Platter

Prepping time: 10 minutes

Cooking time: 8 minutes

Serving: 6

Ingredients:

- 2 tablespoon coconut oil
- 1 tablespoon butter

- 3 garlic cloves, crushed
- 2 teaspoon fresh ginger, grated
- 8 cups red cabbage, shredded
- 1 teaspoon salt
- ½ a teaspoon pepper
- 1/3 cup water

Preparation:

1. Set your Ninja Foodi to Saute mode and add coconut oil and butter, allow to heat up
2. Add garlic and ginger and mix. Add cabbage, pepper, salt, and water
3. Mix well and lock up the lid, cook on HIGH pressure for 5 minutes
4. Perform a quick release and mix. Serve and enjoy!

Nutrition Values Per Serving:

Calories: 96, Fat: 6g, Carbohydrates: 9g, Protein: 1.8g

Very Rich and Creamy Asparagus Soup

Prepping time: 10 minutes

Cooking time: 5-10 minutes

Servings: 4

Ingredients:

- 1 tablespoon olive oil
- 3 green onions, sliced crosswise into ¼ inch pieces
- 1 pound asparagus, tough ends removed, cut into 1 inch pieces
- 4 cups vegetable stock
- 1 tablespoon unsalted butter
- 1 tablespoon almond flour
- 2 teaspoon salt
- 1 teaspoon white pepper
- ½ cup heavy cream

Preparation:

1. Set your Ninja Foodi to "Saute" mode and add oil, let it heat up
2. Add green onions and Saute for a few minutes, add asparagus and stock
3. Lock lid and cook on HIGH pressure for 5 minutes
4. Take a small saucepan and place it over low heat, add butter, flour and stir until the mixture foams and turns into a golden beige, this is your blond roux
5. Remove from heat. Release pressure naturally over 10 minutes
6. Open the lid and add roux, salt, and pepper to the soup
7. Use an immersion blender to puree the soup
8. Taste and season accordingly, swirl in cream and enjoy!

Nutrition Values Per Serving:

Calories: 192, Fat: 14g, Carbohydrates: 8g, Protein: 6g

Fully Stuffed Whole Chicken

Prepping time: 5 minutes

Cooking time: 8 hours

Servings: 4

Ingredients:

- 1 cup mozzarella cheese
- 4 garlic clove, peeled
- 1 whole chicken, 2 pounds, cleaned and dried
- Salt and pepper to taste
- 2 tablespoons lemon juice

Preparation:

1. Stuff chicken cavity with garlic cloves, cheese. Season with salt and pepper
2. Transfer to Ninja Foodi and drizzle lemon juice. Lock lid and SLOW COOK on LOW for 8 hours
3. Transfer to a plate, serve and enjoy!

Nutrition Values Per Serving:

Calories: 309, Fat: 12g, Carbohydrates: 1.6g, Protein: 45g

Delicious Indian Palak Paneer

Prepping time: 10 minutes

Cooking time: 5 minutes

Servings: 4

Ingredients:

- 2 teaspoons olive oil
- 5 garlic cloves, chopped
- 1 tablespoon fresh ginger, chopped
- 1 large yellow onion, chopped
- ½ jalapeno chile, chopped
- 1 pound fresh spinach
- 2 tomatoes, chopped
- 2 teaspoons ground cumin
- ½ teaspoon cayenne
- 2 teaspoons Garam masala
- 1 teaspoon ground turmeric
- 1 teaspoon salt
- ½ cup of water
- 1 and ½ cup paneer cubes
- ½ cup heavy whip cream

Preparation:

1. Pre-heat your Ninja Foodi using Saute mode on HIGH heat, once the pot is hot, add oil and let it shimmer. Add garlic, ginger and chile, Saute for 2-3 minutes
2. Add onion, spinach, tomatoes, cumin, cayenne, garam masala, turmeric, salt, and water
3. Lock lid and cook on HIGH pressure for 2 minutes. Release pressure naturally over 10 minutes
4. Use an immersion blender to puree the mixture to your desired consistency
5. Gently stir in paneer and top with a drizzle of cream. Enjoy!

Nutrition Values Per Serving:

Calories: 185, Fat: 14g, Carbohydrates: 7g, Protein: 7g

Pepper Jack Cauliflower Meal

Prepping time: 5 minutes

Cooking time: 3 hours 35 minutes

Serving: 6

Ingredients:

- 1 head cauliflower
- ¼ cup whipping cream
- 4 ounces cream cheese
- ½ teaspoon pepper
- 1 teaspoon salt
- 2 tablespoons butter
- 4 ounces pepper jack cheese
- 6 bacon slices, crumbled

Preparation:

1. Grease Ninja Foodi and add listed ingredients (except cheese and bacon)
2. Stir and Lock lid, cook SLOW COOK MODE (LOW) for 3 hours
3. Remove lid and add cheese, stir. Lock lid again and cook for 1 hour more
4. Garnish with bacon crumbles and enjoy!

Nutrition Values Per Serving:

Calories: 272, Fat: 21g, Carbohydrates: 5g, Protein: 10g

Well Dressed Brussels

Prepping time: 10 minutes

Cooking time: 4-5 hours

Servings: 4

Ingredients:

- 2 pounds Brussels, halved
- 2 red onions, sliced
- 2 tablespoons apple cider vinegar
- 1 tablespoon extra-virgin olive oil

- 1 teaspoon ground cinnamon
- ½ cup pecans, chopped

Preparation:

1. Add Brussels and onions to Ninja Foodi. Take a small bowl and add cinnamon, vinegar, olive oil
2. Pour mixture over sprouts and toss
3. Place lid and cook on SLOW COOK MODE (LOW) for 4-5 hours. Enjoy!

Nutrition Values Per Serving:

Calories: 176, Fat: 10g, Carbohydrates: 14g, Protein: 4g

Elegant Zero Crust Kale and Mushroom Quiche

Prepping time: 5 minutes

Cooking time: 9 hours

Serving: 6

Ingredients:

- 6 large eggs
- 2 tablespoons unsweetened almond milk
- 2 ounces low –fat feta cheese, crumbled
- ¼ cup parmesan cheese, grated
- 1 and ½ teaspoons Italian seasoning
- 4 ounces mushrooms, sliced
- 2 cups kale, chopped

Preparation:

1. Grease the inner pot of your Ninja Foodi
2. Take a large bowl and whisk in eggs, cheese, almond milk, seasoning and mix it well
3. Stir in kale and mushrooms. Pour the mix into Ninja Foodi. Gently stir
4. Place lid and cook on SLOW COOK Mode(LOW) for 8-9 hours. Serve and enjoy!

Nutrition Values Per Serving:

Calories: 112, Fat: 7g, Carbohydrates: 4g, Protein: 10g

Spicy Cauliflower Steak

Prepping time: 10 minutes

Cooking time: 4 minutes

Serving: 6

Ingredients:

- 1 large head cauliflower
- 2 tablespoon extra-virgin olive oil
- 2 teaspoon paprika
- 2 teaspoon ground cumin
- ¾ teaspoon kosher salt

- 1 cup fresh cilantro, chopped
- 1 lemon, quartered

Preparation:

1. Place the steamer rack into your Ninja Foodi. Add 1 and a ½ cups of water
2. Remove the leaves from the cauliflower and trim the core to ensure that it is able to sit flat
3. Carefully place it on the steam rack. Take a small bowl and add olive oil, cumin, paprika, salt
4. Drizzle the mixture over the cauliflower
5. Lock up the lid and cook on HIGH pressure for 4 minutes
6. Quick release the pressure. Lift the cauliflower to a cutting board and slice into 1-inch steaks
7. Divide the mixture among serving plates and sprinkle with cilantro. Serve and enjoy!

Nutrition Values Per Serving:

Calories: 283, Fats: 19g, Carbs: 18g, Protein: 10g

Thyme and Prosciutto Eggs

Prepping time: 10 minutes

Cooking time: 5 minutes

Servings: 4

Ingredients:

- 4 kale leaves
- 4 prosciutto slices
- 3 tablespoons heavy cream
- 4 hardboiled eggs
- ¼ teaspoon pepper
- ¼ teaspoon salt
- 1 and ½ cups of water

Preparation:

1. Peel eggs and wrap in kale. Wrap in prosciutto and sprinkle salt and pepper
2. Add water to your Ninja Foodi and lower trivet. Place eggs inside and lock lid
3. Cook on HIGH pressure for 5 minutes. Quick release pressure. Serve and enjoy!

Nutrition Values Per Serving:

Calories: 290, Fat: 23g, Carbohydrates: 4g, Protein: 16g

Rosemary Dredged Green Beans

Prepping time: 5 minutes

Cooking time: 3 hours

Servings: 4

Ingredients:

- 1 pound green beans
- 1 tablespoon rosemary, minced

- 1 teaspoon fresh thyme, minced
- 2 tablespoons lemon juice
- 2 tablespoons water

Preparation:

1. Add listed ingredients to Ninja Foodi

2. Lock lid and cook on SLOW COOK MODE(LOW) for 3 hours. Unlock lid and stir. Enjoy!

Nutrition Values Per Serving:

Calories: 40, Fat: 0g, Carbohydrates: 9g, Protein: 2g

Caramelized Onion

Prepping time: 10 minutes

Cooking time: 30-35 minutes

Serving: 6

Ingredients:

- 2 tablespoons unsalted butter
- 3 large onions sliced
- 2 tablespoons water
- 1 teaspoon salt

Preparation:

1. Set your Ninja Foodi to Sauté mode and add set temperature to medium heat, pre-heat the inner pot for 5 minutes. Add butter and let it melt, add onions, water, and stir

2. Lock lid and cook on HIGH pressure for 30 minutes. Quick release the pressure

3. Remove lid and set the pot to sauté mode, let it sear in Medium-HIGH mode for 15 minutes until all liquid is gone. Serve and enjoy!

Nutrition Values Per Serving:

Calories: 283, Fats: 19g, Carbs: 18g, Protein: 10g

Moist Italian Turkey Breast

Prepping time: 5 minutes

Cooking time: 2 hours

Servings: 4

Ingredients:

- 1 and ½ cups Italian dressing
- 2 garlic cloves, minced
- 1 (2 pounds) turkey breast, with bone
- 2 tablespoons butter
- Salt and pepper to taste

Preparation:

1. Mix in garlic cloves, salt, black pepper and rub turkey breast with mix

2. Grease Ninja Foodi pot and arrange turkey breast. Top with Italian dressing
3. Lock lid and BAKE/ROAST for 2 hours at 230 degrees F. Serve and enjoy!

Nutrition Values Per Serving:

Calories: 369, Fat: 23g, Carbohydrates: 6g, Protein: 35g

Cheddar Cauliflower Bowl

Prepping time: 10 minutes

Cooking time: 5 minutes

Servings: 8

Ingredients:

- ¼ cup butter
- ½ sweet onion, chopped
- 1 head cauliflower, chopped
- 4 cups herbed vegetable stock
- ½ teaspoon ground nutmeg
- 1 cup heavy whip cream
- Salt and pepper as needed
- 1 cup cheddar cheese, shredded

Preparation:

1. Set your Ninja Foodi to sauté mode and add butter, let it heat up and melt
2. Add onion and Cauliflower, Saute for 10 minutes until tender and lightly browned
3. Add vegetable stock and nutmeg, bring to a boil
4. Lock lid and cook on HIGH pressure for 5 minutes, quick release pressure once done
5. Remove pot and from Foodi and stir in heavy cream, puree using an immersion blender
6. Season with more salt and pepper and serve with a topping of cheddar. Enjoy!

Nutrition Values Per Serving:

Calories: 227, Fat: 21g, Carbohydrates: 4g, Protein: 8g

Slow-Cooked Brussels

Prepping time: 5 minutes

Cooking time: 4 hours

Servings: 4

Ingredients:

- 1 pound Brussels sprouts, bottom trimmed and cut
- 1 tablespoon olive oil
- 1 -1/2 tablespoon Dijon mustard
- ¼ cup of water
- Salt and pepper as needed
- ½ teaspoon dried tarragon

Preparation:

1. Add Brussels, salt, water, pepper, mustard to Ninja Foodi
2. Add dried tarragon and stir
3. Lock lid and cook on SLOW COOK MODE (LOW) for 5 hours until the Brussels are tender
4. Stir well and add Dijon over Brussels. Stir and enjoy!

Nutrition Values Per Serving:

Calories: 83, Fat: 4g, Carbohydrates: 11g, Protein: 4g

Tasty Cauliflower Soup

Prepping time: 10 minutes

Cooking time: 5 minutes

Servings: 4

Ingredients:

- ½ a small onion, chopped
- 2 tablespoons butter
- 1 large head of cauliflower, leaves and stems removed, coarsely chopped
- 2 cups chicken stock
- 1 teaspoon garlic powder
- 1 teaspoon salt
- 4 ounces cream cheese, cut into cubes
- 1 cup sharp cheddar cheese, cut
- ½ cup cream
- Extra cheddar, sour cream bacon strips, green onion for topping

Preparation:

1. Peel the onion and chop up into small pieces
2. Cut the leaves of the cauliflower and steam, making sure to keep the core intact
3. Coarsely chop the cauliflower into pieces
4. Set your Ninja Foodi to Saute mode and add onion, cook for 2-3 minutes
5. Add chopped cauliflower, stock, salt, and garlic powder
6. Lock up the lid and cook on HIGH pressure for 5 minutes. Perform a quick release
7. Prepare the toppings. Use an immersion blender to puree your soup in the Ninja Foodi
8. Serve your soup with a topping of sliced green onions, cheddar, crumbled bacon. Enjoy!

Nutrition Values Per Serving:

Calories: 438, Fat: 36g, Carbohydrates: 8g, Protein: 22g

Chapter 7-Desserts Recipes

Strawberry-Rhubarb Compote

Prepping time: 10 minutes

Cooking Time: 20 minutes

Servings: 3

Ingredients:

- 2 pound of rhubarb
- ½ a cup of water
- 1 pound of strawberries
- 3 tablespoon of date paste
- Fresh mint

Preparation:

1. Peel rhubarb using a paring knife and chop into ½ inch pieces
2. Add chopped rhubarb to Ninja Food, add water
3. Lock pressure lid and cook on HIGH Pressure for 10 minutes
4. Stem and quarter strawberries and keep them on the side
5. Add strawberries and date paste, stir
6. Lock lid and cook on HIGH Pressure for 20 minutes more
7. Naturally, release the Pressure over 10 minutes
8. Enjoy!

Nutrition Values Per Serving:

Calories: 50, Fat: 2 g, Saturated Fat: 0.5 g, Carbohydrates: 5 g, Fiber: 2 g, Sodium: 9 mg, Protein: 1.4 g

Lemon Mousse Cake

Prepping Time: 15 minutes

Cooking Time: 12 minutes

Servings: 2

Ingredients:

- 4 ounces cream cheese softened
- 1/2 cup heavy cream
- 1/8 cup fresh lemon juice
- 1/2 teaspoon lemon liquid stevia
- 2 pinches salt

Preparation:

1. Take a bowl and mix cream cheese, heavy cream, lemon juice, salt, and stevia.
2. Pour this mixture into the ramekins and transfer the ramekins in the pot of Ninja Foodi.

3. Select "Bake/Roast" and bake for 12 minutes at 350 degrees F.
4. Pour into the serving glasses and refrigerate for at least 3 hours.

Nutrition Values Per Serving:

Calories 305, Total Fat 31 g, Saturated Fat 19.5 g, Cholesterol 103 mg, Sodium 299 mg, Total Carbs 2.7 g, Fiber 0.1 g, Sugar 0.5 g, Protein 5 g

Chocolate Cheesecake

Prepping Time: 15 minutes

Cooking Time: 15 minutes

Servings: 6

Ingredients:

- 2 cups cream cheese, softened
- 2 eggs
- 2 tablespoons cocoa powder
- 1 teaspoon pure vanilla extract
- 1/2 cup Swerve

Preparation:

1. Add eggs, cocoa powder, vanilla extract, swerve, cream cheese in an immersion blender and blend until smooth.
2. Pour the mixture evenly into mason jars.
3. Put the mason jars in the insert of Ninja Foodi and close the lid.
4. Select "Bake/Roast" and bake for 15 minutes at 360 degrees F.
5. Refrigerate for at least 2 hours.

Nutrition Values Per Serving:

Calories 244, Total Fat 24.8 g, Saturated Fat 15.6 g, Cholesterol 32 mg, Sodium 204 mg, Total Carbs 2.1 g, Fiber 0.1 g, Sugar 0.4 g, Protein 4 g

Subtle Potato Gratin

Prepping time: 10 minutes

Cooking Time: 15 minutes

Servings: 3

Ingredients:

- 3 tablespoon of olive oil
- 3 cups of sliced up parsnips
- 3 cloves of garlic, chopped
- 2 cups of vegetable broth
- 1 tablespoon of black pepper
- 1 tablespoon of garlic powder
- 1 cup of mayo

Preparation:

1. Set your Ninja Foodi to Saute mode, add listed ingredients except for mayo
2. Lock lid and cook on HIGH Pressure for 5 minutes
3. Release Pressure naturally over 10 minutes
4. Spread mayo on top, set your Foodi to Saute mode, Low Heat
5. Let it warm
6. Serve and enjoy the gratin!

Nutrition Values Per Serving:

Calories: 201, Fat: 10 g, Saturated Fat: 2 g, Carbohydrates: 22 g, Fiber: 2 g, Sodium: 597 mg, Protein: 6 g

Poached Pear Dessert

Prepping time: 10 minutes

Cooking Time: 10 minutes

Servings: 3

Ingredients:
- 6 firm pears, peeled
- 1 bottle of dry red wine
- 1 bay leaf
- 4 garlic cloves, minced
- 1 stick cinnamon
- 1 fresh ginger, minced
- 1 and 1/3 cup stevia
- Mixed Italian herbs as needed

Preparation:
1. Peel the pears leaving the stems attached
2. Pour wine into your Ninja Foodi
3. Add bay leaf, cinnamon, cloves, ginger, stevia, and stir
4. Add pears to the pot and lock up the lid and cook on HIGH Pressure for 9 minutes
5. Perform a quick release
6. Take the pears out using tong and keep them on the side
7. Set the pot to Saute mode and allow the mixture to reduce to half
8. Drizzle the mixture over the pears and enjoy it!

Nutrition Values Per Serving:

Calories: 150, Fat: 16 g, Saturated Fat: 4 g, Carbohydrates: 2 g, Fiber: 1 g, Sodium:8 mg, Protein: 0.5 g

Coconut and Avocado Pudding

Prepping time: 10 minutes

Cooking Time: 5 minutes

Servings: 4

Ingredients:

- 1 pack, 12 ounces frozen broccoli florets
- 2 tablespoons butter
- salt and pepper as needed
- 8 whole eggs
- 2 tablespoons milk
- ¾ cup white cheddar cheese, shredded
- Crushed red pepper, as needed
- Optional bacon strips

Preparation:

1. Take a bowl and add coconut milk, avocado, vanilla extract, sugar, lime juice, and blend well
2. Pour the mix into a ramekin
3. Add water to your pot
4. Add a steamer basket and place the ramekin in the pot
5. Close lid and cook on HIGH Pressure for 5 minutes
6. Release Pressure naturally over 10 minutes
7. Serve cold and enjoy it!

Nutrition Values Per Serving:

Calories: 190, Fat: 6 g, Saturated Fat: 2 g, Carbohydrates: 6 g, Fiber: 2 g, Sodium: 28 mg, Protein: 4 g

Glazed Carrots

Prepping time: 5 minutes

Cooking Time: 5 minutes

Servings: 4

Ingredients:

- 2 pounds carrots
- Pepper as needed
- 1 cup of water
- 1 tablespoon coconut butter

Preparation:

1. Wash carrots thoroughly and peel then, slice the carrots
2. Add carrots, water to the Ninja Foodi
3. Lock pressure lid and cook for 4 minutes on HIGH Pressure
4. Release pressure naturally
5. Strain carrots and strain carrots
6. Mix with coconut butter, enjoy with a bit of pepper

Nutrition Values Per Serving:

Calories: 228, Fat: 8g, Saturated Fat: 2 g, Carbohydrates: 36g, Fiber: 2 g, Sodium: 123 mg, Protein: 4g

Nut Porridge

Prepping Time: 15 minutes

Cooking Time: 10 minutes

Servings: 4

Ingredients:

- 4 teaspoons coconut oil, melted
- 1 cup pecans, halved
- 2 cups of water
- 2 tablespoons stevia
- 1 cup cashew nuts, raw and unsalted

Preparation:

1. Put the cashew nuts and pecans in the precision processor and pulse till they are in chunks.
2. Put this mixture into the pot of Ninja Foodi and stir in water, coconut oil and stevia.
3. Select sauté on Ninja Foodi and cook for 15 minutes.
4. Serve and enjoy.

Nutrition Values Per Serving:

Calories 260, Total Fat 22.9 g, Saturated Fat 7.3 g, Cholesterol 0 mg, Sodium 9 mg, Total Carbs 12.7 g, Fiber 1.4 g, Sugar 1.8 g, Protein 5.6 g

Peanut Butter Cups

Prepping Time: 15 minutes

Cooking Time: 30 minutes

Servings: 3

Ingredients:

- 1 cup butter
- 1/4 cup heavy cream
- 2 ounces unsweetened chocolate
- 1/4 cup peanut butter, separated
- 4 packets stevia

Preparation:

1. Mix well and pour the mixture in a baking mold.
2. Put the baking mold in the Ninja Foodi and press "Bake/Roast."
3. Set the timer for 30 minutes at 360 degrees F and dish out to serve.

Nutrition Values Per Serving:

Calories 479, Total Fat 51.5 g, Saturated Fat 29.7 g, Cholesterol 106 mg, Sodium 69 mg, Total Carbs 7.7 g, Fiber 2.7 g, Sugar 1.4 g, Protein 5.2 g

Carrot and Pumpkin Pudding

Prepping time: 10 minutes

Cooking Time: 20 minutes

Servings: 3

Ingredients:

- 1 tablespoon extra-virgin olive oil
- 2 cups carrots, shredded
- 2 cups pureed pumpkin
- ½ sweet onion, finely chopped
- 1 cup heavy whip cream
- ½ cup cream cheese, soft
- 2 whole eggs
- 1 tablespoon brown sugar
- 1 teaspoon ground nutmeg
- ½ teaspoon salt
- ¼ cup pumpkin seeds, garnish
- A ¼ cup of water

Preparation:

1. Add oil to your Ninja Foodi pot and whisk well
2. Add carrots, pumpkin, onion, heavy cream cheese, eggs, sugar, salt, and water
3. Mix well
4. Lock lid and cook on HIGH Pressure for 10 minutes
5. Release Pressure naturally over 10 minutes
6. Top with pumpkin seeds and serve
7. Enjoy!

Nutrition Values Per Serving:

Calories: 239, Fat: 19 g, Saturated Fat: 2 g, Carbohydrates: 7 g, Fiber: 2 g, Sodium: 79 mg, Protein: 6 g

Vanilla Yogurt

Prepping Time: 15 minutes

Cooking Time: 3 hours

Servings: 2

Ingredients:

- 1/2 cup full-fat milk
- 1/4 cup yogurt starter
- 1 cup heavy cream
- 1/2 tablespoon pure vanilla extract
- 2 scoops stevia

Preparation:

1. Add milk, heavy cream, vanilla extract, and stevia in Ninja Foodi.
2. Let yogurt sit and press "slow cooker" and set the timer to 4 hours on "low."
3. Add yogurt starter in 1 cup of milk.
4. Return this mixture to the pot.
5. Close the lid and wrap the Ninja Foodi in small towels.
6. Let yogurt sit for about 9 hours.
7. Dish out, refrigerate and then serve.

Nutrition Values Per Serving:

Calories 292, Total Fat 26.2 g, Saturated Fat 16.3 g, Cholesterol 100 mg, Sodium 86 mg, Total Carbs 8.2 g, Fiber 0 g, Sugar 6.6 g, Protein 5.2 g

Amazing Chocolate Brownies

Prepping Time: 15 minutes

Cooking Time: 32 minutes

Servings: 4

Ingredients:

- 3 eggs
- 1/2 cup butter
- 1/2 cup sugar-free chocolate chips
- 2 scoops stevia
- 1 teaspoon vanilla extract

Preparation:

1. Take a bowl and mix eggs, stevia, and vanilla extract.
2. Pour this mixture in the blender and blend until smooth.
3. Sauté for 2 minutes until the chocolate is melted.
4. Add the melted chocolate into the egg mixture.
5. Press "Bake/Roast" and set the timer for about 30 minutes at 360 degrees F.
6. Bake for about 30 minutes, cut into pieces and serve.

Nutrition Values Per Serving:

Calories 266, Total Fat 26.9 g, Saturated Fat 15.8 g, Cholesterol 184 mg, Sodium 218 mg, Total Carbs 2.5 g, Fiber 0 g, Sugar 0.4 g, Protein 4.5 g

Lemon Mousse

Prepping time: 10 minutes

Cooking Time: 12 minutes

Servings: 2

Ingredients:

- 1-2 ounces cream cheese, soft

- ½ cup heavy cream
- 1/8 cup fresh lemon juice
- ½ teaspoon lemon liquid stevia
- 2 pinch salt

Preparation:

1. Take a bowl and mix in cream cheese, heavy cream, lemon juice, salt, and stevia
2. Pour mixture into a ramekin and transfer to Ninja Foodi
3. Lock lid and choose the Bake/Roast mode and bake for 12 minutes at 350 degrees F
4. Check using a toothpick if it comes out clean
5. Serve and enjoy!

Nutrition Values Per Serving:

Calories: 290, Fat: 26 g, Saturated Fat: 4 g, Carbohydrates: 8 g, Fiber: 2 g, Sodium: 23 mg, Protein: 5 g

Delicious Pot-De-Crème

Prepping time: 10 minutes

Cooking Time: 20 minutes

Servings: 3

Ingredients:

- 6 egg yolks
- 2 cups heavy whip cream
- 1/3 cup cocoa powder
- 1 tablespoon pure vanilla extract
- ½ teaspoon liquid stevia
- Whipped coconut cream for garnish
- Shaved dark chocolate for garnish

Preparation:

1. Take a medium-sized bowl and whisk in yolks, heavy cream, sugar, cocoa powder, vanilla
2. Pour mixture in 1 and ½ quart baking dish, stir
3. Transfer the mix to Ninja Foodi basket
4. Add water to about the halfway point of the ramekin
5. Lock lid and cook on HIGH Pressure for 12 minutes
6. Quick-release pressure, remove the baking dish and let it cool
7. Let it chill in the fridge
8. Garnish with coconut cream, add chocolate shavings
9. Serve and enjoy!

Nutrition Values Per Serving:

Calories: 258, Fat: 18 g, Saturated Fat: 3 g, Carbohydrates: 3 g, Fiber: 3 g, Sodium: 146 mg, Protein: 5 g

Made in the USA
Monee, IL
09 March 2021